YOU CAN FIGHT VARICOSE VEINS—AND WIN!

Today, many doctors believe that the onset of varicose veins can be predicted and controlled. New attention is being paid to the roles of diet, exercise, heredity, and pregnancy. With this new understanding, patients can minimize their risk of developing the problem or control its progress.

The purpose of this book is to describe how modern medicine treats varicosities; to tell you about some things you can do to prevent or minimize their occurence; to describe the many products, resources and treatment facilities available; and most important, to make all this information available to you in a way you can really use.

It is estimated that nearly 1 in 4 people in this country suffer from varicose veins at some point in their lives. It's time that they had enough information to understand their condition and do something about it. That's why this book was written.

NO MORE VARICOSE VEINS

LUIS NAVARRO, M.D.,
NANCY S. MILLER AND
STEPHEN KLING

BANTAM BOOKS
NEW YORK · TORONTO · LONDON · SYDNEY · AUCKLAND

NO MORE VARICOSE VEINS
A Bantam Book / October 1988

ISBN 0-553-27224-1

Published simultaneously in the United States and Canada

Bantam Books are published by Bantam Books, a division of Bantam Doubleday Dell Publishing Group, Inc. Its trademark, consisting of the words ''Bantam Books'' and the portrayal of a rooster, is Registered in U.S. Patent and Trademark Office and in other countries. Marca Registrada. Bantam Books, 666 Fifth Avenue, New York, New York 10103.

PRINTED IN THE UNITED STATES OF AMERICA

AUTHOR'S NOTE

The information contained in this book is intended to complement, not replace, the advice of your own physician, with whom you should always consult before starting any medical treatment, diet or exercise program. Only your personal physician can give you the individual medical counseling that you need.

For sharing love and for the life
Which all three help enthrall,
To D.T.M. and S.A.L.
and KUKY most of all.

L.N.

CONTENTS

INTRODUCTION

Y ou have, or someone you know has, varicose veins.* Otherwise you wouldn't be reading this book.

You might not rank them with the most serious medical problems (they're usually not) and most people don't give them much thought. But to sufferers of this unsightly affliction, varicose veins are more than a minor cosmetic problem. People who have varicose veins, or their smaller cousins, "spider" veins, know what it's like to be embarrassed: while wearing bathing suits or Bermuda shorts; on the beach or at the gym; and in so many other situations that other people take for granted.

Varicose vein sufferers often live secret lives. Many think up elaborate subterfuges to avoid exposing their varicosities to friends, colleagues, even spouses. One

---

*"Varicose veins," as we use the term here, refer to any visible vein problem—from the tiniest "broken capillaries," or "spider" veins, to the large, knotty, painful, *true* varicose veins.

woman—stylish, successful, not yet forty—adopted a designer wardrobe entirely in black, orchestrated around an ever-present pair of black tights. None of her friends knew that there was any reason behind her ''look'' other than her love of high fashion. But she'd suffered from varicose veins for years. Her wardrobe was her only solution. She never swam, never played tennis, never went to the beach, never went anywhere her black tights couldn't go. No one knew how miserable she was.

Men also suffer in silence, though less frequently. For them it's usually not the unsightliness of varicose veins that drives them to look for help. One man, a clothing designer, spent long hours every day standing in front of his drawing table, rarely moving from that one spot. (That's a classic way to speed up the development of varicose veins, as you'll learn later.) After a few years of this, when varicose veins appeared, it was the pain and stiffness that made him notice them. But he didn't seek treatment at first. He endured the pain until his legs hurt so much he couldn't stand anymore. Only when the pain became unbearable and complications appeared (his veins started to bleed—as *can* happen with advanced cases) did he seek treatment.

There are probably some things you already know about varicose veins—things you've been told, things you've read in magazines, things you've heard from friends trying to be helpful. Maybe you've gone for treatment already, or maybe going for treatment simply never occurred to you. Maybe you—like so many millions of people around the world—don't know that treatment is available at all. Or maybe you thought that treatment would be more painful, disfiguring, and traumatic than varicose veins themselves.

For a problem as widespread as varicose veins (it's

estimated that 25 percent of all women and 10 percent of all men are affected by the disease), it's astounding how little people know about them, apart from the fact that they're ugly, occasionally painful, and won't go away by themselves. Often what people do know about varicose veins is outdated, almost useless information, gleaned from well-meaning (but ignorant) friends or acquaintances.

Even doctors aren't necessarily reliable sources on the latest approaches. Methods of treatment of varicose veins can vary enormously from area to area, depending on local customs as much as on modern procedures. If Dr. White of Anytown, USA, has been treating varicose veins in a certain way for the last forty years, it's not unlikely that Drs. Black, Brown, and Green of the same town treat them in much the same way.

Why don't people find out the real story? Maybe because people think no one ever died from varicose veins. (Not true.[1]) Or maybe they think that the major complaint of most sufferers has to do with their appearance. (That **is** true.) Or maybe the embarrassment of having varicose veins discourages potential patients from finding out about them.

Whatever the reason, the fact is that ignorance and misinformation are so widespread that most people don't understand the first thing about varicose veins, why they happen, and what they **can** do about them.

But what are varicose veins? What causes them? Why do some people develop them, while others don't? These questions have been puzzling physicians almost since the beginning of written history.

Not too long ago—just several hundred years, in fact—doctors had little idea about what the blood system was, or how it worked. The circulatory system in general, and veins in particular, were a puzzle. Varicose veins were a fairly common problem, but their origins were mysterious. Treatment consisted of rather drastic measures, which did little to improve the patient's appearance, or their health. Sometimes the patient looked worse after treatment than before. Sometimes the "cure" was fatal.

There is evidence that the ancient Egyptians, at the time of the Pharaohs, knew about varicosities and tried to treat them. Hippocrates, the great Greek philosopher and physician, wrote about possible treatments for varicose veins more than 2,500 years ago.[2] Centuries later, the renowned anatomist Galen offered his idea of treatment: tear the veins out with hooks. (Fortunately, this never caught on.) In the days of the Romans, in the Dark Ages, and in the Renaissance, right up to relatively recent modern medicine in the middle of the nineteenth century, varicose veins appeared prominently as one of the problems everyone tried to solve, but with little success. Indeed, reading a treatise on these ancient recommended therapies is like reading a textbook on torture.

By the middle of the nineteenth century, medical men began to decipher some of the questions about circulation and veins. At the same time, important advances were being made in the area of surgical techniques, anesthesia, and disinfectants. The hypodermic needle was invented. This new knowledge and these instruments led to the first procedures to treat varicose veins more safely than before.

Progress continued steadily into the beginning of the twentieth century. It's only in the last fifty years that the age-old ailment of varicosities has been truly understood and treated with good results. And most important for today's patient, doctors have finally realized that sufferers of varicose veins are just as interested in the way their veins look as in the way their veins work.

The fact is, most people who seek treatment do so for cosmetic reasons. And advanced—truly advanced—techniques have made treatments better, faster, and safer, yielding excellent results with a minimum of discomfort.

Treatments have been refined to the point that even the tiny spider veins, which rarely (if ever) have any serious medical impact, can now be eliminated with hardly a trace. And the more serious cases of varicose veins are treatable with sophisticated techniques that are more cosmetically pleasing than ever before. So, while suffering from varicose veins has never been easy, today there's more hope and promise—and results—than at any other time in history.

Varicose veins are not hard to miss. They're usually blue or purple, often knotty or gnarled, and almost always in the lower legs, along the backs of the calves or along the inside of the knee. They can extend all the way to the groin, or they can start and end in no particular place. They're often accompanied by tiny, threadlike spider veins, which may or may not be a related condition. If varicose veins are ignored, they can cause discoloration to the tissues around them, and if they're left without treatment for long enough, they can lead to swelling, bleeding, and—in serious cases—ulceration of the skin that can prove very difficult to heal. And varicose veins can ache—a heavy, dull pain that grows as the day wears on—and can cause cramps at night.

Of course, every purplish blotch or spot is not a varicose vein. The body often bruises or discolors for other reasons, like simple bumps or sprains. And every pain isn't a varicose vein, either. Some pain may be nothing more serious than a twinge of arthritis or a muscle ache, but some could be a warning sign of a more worrisome illness: bone and joint problems, serious arterial deficiencies, or even back problems.

No one gets varicose veins overnight. It's a progressive disease that takes years and years to develop, and then more years to turn into anything more serious than ugly bluish lines on the legs. They are not life-threatening, unless they are totally ignored for a very long time. Today many doctors believe that the onset of varicose veins can be to some extent predicted and controlled. New attention is being paid to the roles of diet, exercise, heredity, and pregnancy. With this new understanding of the causes of varicosities, perhaps patients can live their lives in ways that minimize their risk of developing the problem or control its progress.

The purpose of this book is fivefold: **first**, to educate you about the human body's workings so that you can understand a little about the causes of varicose veins; **second**, to describe how modern medicine treats varicosities of all kinds. **Third**, we'll tell you about some things you can do to prevent or minimize their occurrence. **Fourth**, we'll describe the many products, resources, and treatment facilities available in the United States and tell you how to find out about them. And **fifth**, and most important, we'll try to make all this information available to you in a way you can really understand and use.

It is estimated that nearly one in four people in this country suffer from varicose veins at some point in their lives. Isn't it time that those people have enough information to understand their condition and do something about it? That's why this book was written.

PART I

WHAT ARE VARICOSE VEINS?

CHAPTER 1

THE ANATOMY
AND PHYSIOLOGY
OF VARICOSE VEINS

Varicose veins are a uniquely human disease. As far as we know, no other creature in the animal kingdom suffers from this condition. Most of the reason for this is that man is the only mammal to walk on two legs, and the design of the circulatory system being what it is, only man has to pump most of his blood around **vertically**. Dogs and cats, lions, bears, and monkeys are primarily horizontal creatures, and their circulatory systems pump the bulk of their blood horizontally, sidestepping the wearing effects of gravity. Man (or woman) is not so fortunate; the force of gravity naturally tends to pull our blood down to the lowest points in our bodies: our feet and lower legs.

This is why, to a large degree, varicose veins occur mostly in the legs, and within the legs, mostly below the knee. Of all the blood vessels in the body, the legs' vessels do the toughest duty because gravity causes blood to pool in them. Imagine filling a garden hose with water, then holding the nozzle end up, away from the ground. The downward force of gravity would naturally pull the water down toward the lowest point in the hose. The same principle is at work in your veins.

The blood pressure in our feet is always higher than the blood pressure in our heads, due to gravity. Without the aid of our muscles to send the blood back, it would tend to collect there, causing swelling and a feeling of heavy sluggishness.

Here's an illustration that most of us can recognize: ever notice when you first wake up in the morning how your face is swollen and red, often just on the side you were sleeping on? Because your facial muscles (as well as most others in your body) are inactive while you sleep, the blood in the veins in that area is not being sent efficiently along its way. The force of gravity causes the blood to collect and pool at the lowest points of your face, giving you that grumpy-looking puffy face in the morning.

Because the veins in your legs are the farthest away from the heart, they get the least help from the heart in propelling the blood back to where it came from. But before you can really understand why you have varicose veins, you need to understand a little about how your body's circulatory system works. It's not complicated; it's a wonderfully diverse system that depends on a few simple principles. Once you understand those few principles, you can much better understand why varicose veins happen the way they do. And that's the first step toward doing something about them.

Let's start at the beginning.

Most people know that the heart is a small but powerful pump that propels blood through a miraculously complex system of blood vessels to every single cell throughout every part of the body. Put all the blood vessels in your body end to end and they'd go around the world twice, and you'd still have enough to go cross-country again—more than 51,000 miles of arteries, veins, and capillaries.

The blood vessels themselves are marvels of engineering. They form a vast network throughout your entire body, piping fresh blood through the largest, most powerful arteries to the tiniest microscopic threads of capillaries.

But the blood vessels are more than just plumbing. They regulate the temperature of the body by opening up (to cool you off) or closing down (to keep you warm). They express deep feelings, too: When the vessels open up in your face, that's a blush; when you're mad, you flush. As the vessels expand, blood flows faster to those areas that might need it most—to the muscles, for example, during strenuous physical activity, or even to the brain during deep thought.

Some blood vessels in effect, store extra blood. When your body needs extra blood for a particular area or organ, the blood is released. When you're quiet, some blood is taken back into these vessels in a kind of reserve, to wait for the next time it's needed.

Your blood carries nutrients—oxygen, water, food, minerals—to each cell and, after each drop of blood brings its tiny load of fresh supplies, it carries away from the cell the waste materials, then returns to the heart and lungs to pick up another fresh load for the next trip around. Without our circulatory systems, we'd still be one-celled organisms living in pond water; our bodies could never live, grow, or flourish.

Let's take a closer look at how the mechanical parts of the circulatory system work together, by following your blood's circuit around the body.

From your heart, blood moves through very large arteries to the distant parts of your body. The heart beats seventy times a minute for as many as seventy-five years or more, pumping 1½ gallons of blood each of those minutes. Sixty million gallons in an average lifetime. Nearly three **billion** heartbeats.

Like the water in your plumbing system at home, the blood system is pressurized. That's the main force that keeps it moving with each heartbeat. "Blood pressure" is a term describing how much pressure there is in the circulatory system. It's important for our bodies to maintain the right blood pressure; too little pressure means that there is not sufficient *oomph* behind the blood to keep it efficiently moving to all the parts of the body that might need it. Too much pressure is also a problem—it can seriously damage the delicate structures inside our organs and blood vessels.

The largest of the circulatory system's blood vessels are called arteries; they are the "pipes" that lead directly out of the heart. (**Arteries** carry fresh blood **away** from the heart, while the vessels that bring spent and depleted blood **back** to the heart for replenishing are called **veins**. There is one important exception to this rule, but we'll talk about that in a minute.) These arteries are not merely hollow tubes. They're strong, muscular organs that actually pump along with the heart to keep the blood pressurized. Throughout the arterial part of the circulatory system, the arteries gently pulsate along with every heartbeat.

From the largest arteries, the blood travels into smaller arteries. The entire arterial system keeps branching out and branching out, with the arteries getting smaller and smaller with each junction, until there are literally millions of these blood vessels carrying fresh blood to each and every individual cell. The smallest arteries are called arterial capillaries, and they are so small that even the tiny red blood cells that make up the blood and carry all the fresh oxygen and nutrients—themselves so small that they can only be seen with a powerful microscope—must pass through single file.

At the individual cell, the exchange of fresh supplies for expended supplies takes place. As the blood gives up its load of oxygen and nutrients, it takes back carbon dioxide, salts and acids, and the other by-products of life. The blood changes from its bright red color to a darker bluish tint.

It's at this point that the blood enters the venous system and begins its route back to the heart to be replenished.

The venous system is made up of blood vessels that range from the tiniest capillary-size veins to the larger and ever-larger sized blood vessels that mirror the branchings of the arterial system. The closer the veins get to the heart, the bigger they get, with the vena cava, the largest of the veins, passing blood directly to the heart.

After the depleted blood arrives back at the heart, it's pumped into the lungs to be replenished with oxygen. This is the only place in the body where depleted blood is pumped by an artery (to the lungs), and returns (to the heart) bright red and fresh, inside a vein.

Now the blood is ready for another round trip.

VEINS

Veins differ from arteries in several important respects. Veins are not muscular organs. (They do have a little muscle tissue, but not nearly as much as arteries.) They are much more like hollow tubes. In veins, the pressure that drives blood through the circulatory system is very much reduced. (That's why an injury to a vein is not generally as serious or life-threatening as an injury to an artery. When an artery is torn or cut, the pressure of the blood causes it to spurt out very quickly, pulsating with the heartbeat. In contrast, an injury to a vein bleeds more slowly, in a steady, nonpulsating flow.) Many veins lie very close to the surface of your skin; you can easily see the bluish lines they trace in your arms or legs, even if they are not varicose. Arteries are not usually visible, because they are protected from injury by muscles and bones.

The veins move with a different rhythm than the arteries just on the "other side of the fence." Whereas the arterial system moves quickly and steadily, powered by the irresistible pulsating force of the heart—pumping, pumping, beat after beat, day in and day out—the venous system pokes along more slowly and calmly. In this part of the circulatory system, the heartbeat is quite faint. Blood pressure is reduced. The speed of the blood, too, is slowed down.

Veins have several functions, besides just returning blood to the heart. When we spoke of the blood vessels that help to store extra reserves of blood until they're needed, we were speaking about veins. Go jogging and these reserves drop; the blood is called out and sent to the legs, as well as to other muscles. And when we spoke about the body's thermostat—opening to cool us down, and closing to warm us up—we were also talking about veins, which work in conjunction with the arteries. On a hot day our skin can flush as the veins seek to disperse the excess heat our bodies are generating. On a cold day, these veins close down to conserve heat—that's why your hands and feet get so cold in winter.

The most important force moving the blood through the veins—though not as strong as in the arteries—is still the **heart**. The vein walls do not pulsate with every heartbeat, but the substantial force of the blood pressure is still there driving the blood forward, albeit a good deal more slowly and gently. Doctors call this residual heart force *vis a tergo*, a Latin term that means the "force from behind."

But there are other forces moving the blood through the veins. Not as important as the heartbeat, but essential nevertheless, is the **"muscle pump"**; that is, to a large degree the muscles themselves power the venous system and move the blood smoothly along. The veins lie close to the muscles in your body. Either they're on top of them, just under the skin, or they're deep on the inside, near your bones. Some veins straddle the fence— they penetrate the muscles and take blood from the superficial veins to the deep veins. (These veins are called perforators because they perforate the muscles. We'll talk about perforators again, because they figure importantly in the development of varicose veins.)

Think of it: Every time you move a muscle in your body, whether you're walking, running, scratching your nose, or just talking on the telephone, the muscles involved in that activity are flexing and tensing, then relaxing, and then tensing again. As they contract and expand, they squeeze the thin-walled veins that lie near them ever so slightly. The repeated squeezings and contractions squirt the blood in those veins forward.

A classic illustration of the muscles' relationship with the venous system is the case of the soldier standing in formation for long hours without any movement. There's a complex interplay of forces that can occur, standing on the drill field in the hot sun. Basically, with no muscular activity to aid in circulating blood back to the heart (and afterward to the brain and other sensitive organs), the blood pools in the lowest parts of the body and the soldier can collapse in a dead faint. He recovers when he's dragged off the drill field, mostly because the prone position allows blood from the lower extremities to flow back to the heart.

The third force that helps the blood return to the

heart is the **negative pressure** created in your chest when you inhale. All this means is that as you breathe an area of lower pressure in your chest cavity naturally tends to draw the blood toward it. It's a subtle force, but it's there.

If you were to chart the relative importance of these various blood-moving forces, the action of the heart would be at the top, the muscle pump in the middle, and the negative pressure of the chest cavity would be way at the bottom.

As mentioned above, some veins—the ones you can see in your forearms or along the backs of your knees, for instance—lie close to the surface of your skin. These are called superficial veins. They are generally smaller vessels that collect blood from their immediate surroundings and pipeline it to larger veins deep inside your muscles. The superficial veins range from tiny capillary-size vessels up to larger, more important veins, as we'll see later. But they always empty into a much larger vein that's part of the "deep" system.

Underneath your first few layers of skin and fat, there's a membrane—a tough, flexible sheath of semi-transparent tissue—that separates the superficial veins from the deep system veins. Any vein on the outside of this sheath is called superficial, any vein on the inside is called deep. The connecting veins, those that run from the skin down through the muscle sheath into the deep veins, are the perforators. It's a distinction that may not seem important to you now, but when we actually discuss varicose veins, you'll see that it's only the superficial veins that become truly varicose, often with some involvement of the perforators. If the deep system veins fail, it's a much more serious problem.

Deep system veins are the major thoroughfare of the venous part of the circulatory system. They are large, thin-walled vessels, so they're quite fragile. They're buried deep within the body to protect them from injury, next to the bones, near the arteries. The deep system veins get larger and larger as they converge closer and closer to the heart, until they all meet in the vena cava, which funnels the blood into the heart.

VALVES AND VARICOSE VEINS

We've talked now about the kinds of structures veins are, and about the kinds of forces that push the blood along, back to the heart. But we've left out one very important detail. And it's this one detail that is crucial when it comes to explaining varicose veins.

Here's an easy way to understand the principle behind this next piece of the puzzle: imagine you've got a length of garden hose, a few feet long. It's not connected to a faucet or a nozzle; it's just lying in front of you on the ground. For the purposes of this example it's half full of water.

Pretend you're a muscle, and this length of garden hose is the vein that runs nearby. When you step on the center of the hose, you're applying the same kind of force that a real muscle applies to a real vein.

Let's watch what happens.

You step hard in the center of the hose, and the water squirts out—both ends at once.

If you were a real muscle, and the hose was a real vein, it's easy to see that this would not be a very effective way to get the blood—the water in this simple example—to flow in the one direction it must go to get to the heart.

What to do? An engineer would solve the problem

the same way your body does: by adding valves along the length of the hose—valves that allow the flow to go in one direction only.

The main veins in your legs have ten to twenty such tiny valves—one every few inches. They're a little like the locks on a canal. They allow the vein to fill up one section at a time, always moving the blood closer to the heart and preventing the blood from flowing backward, down toward the feet. These valves appear in veins all through your body, but most of them are found in the legs, because the veins in the legs are so long.

The valves are surprisingly simple structures: two flaps of a muscular membranous tissue that meet in an inverted V. It doesn't take much to squeeze the blood up through the valve; the point of the V opens up when pressure is applied, then snaps shut, so the blood can't trickle back through in the other direction.

At least that's the way these tiny valves were designed to function. But, for a variety of reasons—and we'll go into those soon—something occasionally happens to the structure of a tiny valve that causes it to fail. It swings open when force is applied from either direction, and the orderly, well-engineered flow back to the heart falters. The blood moving slowly up toward the heart from the legs falls back down where it came from. That blood then pools at the next valve down the road, causing a bottleneck in the traffic flow, and that bottleneck might be the beginning of a varicose vein.

Don't forget that blood has weight. If one tiny valve fails, that means the healthy valve below now has to do double duty. It must hold not only its share of blood (until the next muscle contraction squeezes the blood along the vein), it must also hold the next valve's share. Year in and year out, this means greater wear and tear on the healthy valve. It may fail, too.

Now we have a chain reaction. The second valve

has failed, depositing its load of blood on the third valve down the line. Gravity is a relentless force, and the healthy third valve has a triple load of blood to keep from falling back toward the ground. How long can this valve hold on?

Maybe you remember an old sight gag that animated cartoons used to use occasionally. The hapless hero crashes through the roof of a house, then through the floor of the top floor, then through the next floor, and then through the floor below that. Eventually, he hits the basement. That, in metaphorical form, is what can happen to a vein.

The result of this situation is not as funny as the cartoon, as is well known to anybody who suffers from varicose veins. The vein becomes enlarged and distended as these excess quantities of blood—greater than the vein was designed to handle—pool and collect. The vein itself balloons out like an overinflated automobile tire. Even more blood collects in the distorted area, and the vein becomes visible, discolored with the blue-purple tinge of deoxygenated blood.

It's not that the color of a varicose vein is any different from that of a healthy vein, it's just that the vein distorts, fills up with even more blood, and rises closer to the surface of the skin, so it can be seen all the more.

The distortion caused by the excess blood causes even more valves to fail as the flaps of the valves are forced farther and farther apart. The varicosity worsens until all the symptoms of varicose veins are present: the discomfort, the cramps, the ugly blue lines that seem to pop out of your skin. If nothing is done to treat the vein, complications can appear.

Once this has occurred, there is nothing you can do to make this varicose vein function again. It won't go away by itself, no matter how much you want it to.

And if you leave it untreated, it will inevitably get worse. But there are things you can do—concrete, real solutions—to correct developing varicosities, and to treat and eliminate the varicosities that have gone unchecked, **if** you know how to identify the warning signs of varicose veins.

CHAPTER 2

WHAT CAUSES VARICOSE VEINS?

No one really knows.

People have suffered from varicose veins throughout recorded history, but science has yet to figure out why this most common of circulatory problems happens.

The basic puzzle is the arbitrariness with which varicose veins appear. We can point to several conditions that seem to lead to varicose veins in some people—for instance, physical inactivity and poor muscle tone. But the fact is, two people can work side by side for most of their lives in similarly inactive desk jobs—with most details of their lives, including the number of hours they sit hovering over their paperwork, nearly identical—and only one of them might develop varicose veins. And while physical inactivity is a cause we can single out with some confidence, the paradox is that some athletes who engage in nothing **but** intense physical activity also develop varicose veins—even as (or maybe because) they transform their bodies into sculptured muscular marvels.

Whereas most varicose veins have no obvious cause,

some varicose veins—a tiny percentage of the total—**do** have a definite, identifiable cause. These are called ''secondary varicose veins'' and are usually caused by a disease, an injury, a congenital malformation, or some other form of blockage in the venous system. We'll mention them again at length. They differ from the kind most people get.

But the average, run-of-the-mill varicose veins— primary varicose veins—are not caused by anything sinister. Primary varicosities are of indefinite origin, caused not by disease or trauma but, we think, by many subtle factors. These primary varicose veins are the focus of this book.

ONE CAUSE OF VARICOSE VEINS MAY BE CIVILIZATION

Varicose veins, though with us since the time we descended from the trees and walked upright, have become more prevalent in mankind since the advent of the industrial revolution. Even today, researchers note a far lower incidence of varicosities in primitive peoples who live by hunting or subsistence farming.

Why? Theories abound. Some of them are more obvious than others: Those living in the wild get more exercise during their lives, chasing antelope or scratching out a living from the earth. Maybe greater physical activity in these cultures has kept varicose veins away.

Third World diets are much higher in fiber and lower in protein, some researchers say. Civilization has made us soft and our diets too rich, too refined. You'll see later that there is indeed a link between diet and varicose veins. The less bulk and fiber in the diet, the greater likelihood there is (in *some* people) that varicose veins will develop.

One of the more intriguing theories of what causes varicose veins cites one of civilization's most mundane contributions as a principal culprit: the chair. Could sitting in chairs be the cause of varicose veins in modern man? Dr. Colin James Alexander, a New Zealand doctor, recently advanced this hypothesis based on evidence that Eastern and primitive cultures suffer from varicose veins far less than Western man. We in the industrialized world sit for hours in chairs—some of us spend as much as one third of our lives sitting in chairs—which may interfere with the body's main circulatory mechanisms by weakening development of the veins' walls, starting in childhood. Many primitive peoples sit, or crouch, on the ground. Their vein walls grow to be stronger and therefore resistant to the forces that can cause varicose veins. If this theory turns out to be true, then perhaps varicose veins are entirely preventable—if one doesn't mind spending one's life sitting on the floor.[3]

PEOPLE GENERALLY DEVELOP VARICOSE VEINS AS THEY AGE

As we grow older, our bodies tend to lose elasticity. Our skin becomes dry and wrinkled, eyesight can suffer, joints can ache. Varicose veins often seem to be just another sign of getting old.

The incidence of varicose veins increases in direct relationship to the age of the patient. To some degree, varicose veins are a symptom of wear and tear on the body, since they occur primarily in the legs, and the veins in our legs do the heaviest duty of all the veins. They are not only the farthest from the heart, but they're also the longest veins, and the sheer weight of the column of blood they support is greater than that of any other vein. So the wear and tear on these veins is considerably greater than on any others.

Primary varicose veins are rare in people under 25 (with the exception of women who have gone through multiple childbirths, and in the rare cases of some congenital defects). Doctors aren't sure why a correlation exists between age and varicosities, but it does. Perhaps it takes a certain number of years for valve problems to crop up, or perhaps it has to do with changing amounts of hormones in your body as you age. There are theories that the elasticity of veins lessens as you grow older; this means that your veins are less and less able to "bounce back" from increased pressures and stresses.

Statistics about varicose vein sufferers seem to support this: At age 30, 19% of men and 44% of women have noticed some beginning signs of varicosities. (There are several reasons for the dramatic difference in these percentages between the sexes. First, men don't seem to notice their varicose veins as much as women do. Maybe, as some doctors say, they just aren't as sensitive to the way they look. More likely, though, it's got to do with the hair men have on their legs; it can hide a lot of the disfigurement. Second, and more important, it's pregnancy that to a large degree brings on varicose veins in younger women. More on that soon. These percentages increase with age. At 40, 23.5% of men and 54% of women are affected; by age 50, 42% of men and 64% of women have some form of varicose veins.[4]

THE TENDENCY TO DEVELOP VARICOSE VEINS IS INHERITED

Some people are just predisposed to develop varicose veins.

Some people are predisposed not to.

Of all the contributing circumstances in the development of varicose veins, heredity seems to play the biggest part. Why this hereditary link exists remains a mystery, however. Evidence shows that there seem to be "constitutional defects" in the structure of the veins and valves of those predisposed, and that these "defects" might be passed on from generation to generation. Perhaps, some researchers say, there is an inherited weakness in a specific gene that governs the development of veins.

There is evidence that some patients are missing a layer of muscular tissue in the veins themselves. While veins are not particularly muscular organs, there is some muscle present, especially near the valves—or there should be. Is the muscle missing from birth in these patients, or does some abnormal atrophy occur over the course of years? We are not sure.

Varicose veins do seem to have a different chemical makeup from that of normal veins. Collagen, the strong fiberlike material that is a building block of many of the body's toughest components (like tendons, bones, and cartilage), is also an important building block of veins. It serves the same sort of function as the steel in a steel belted tire, but researchers have found it to be in short supply in varicose veins. Is this lack an inherited tendency? No one knows for sure.[5]

Strangely enough, some sufferers of varicose veins don't have very many valves in their veins, and that could be a contributing factor, too. The number of valves (and their exact placement) normally varies from person to person. The fewer valves there are, the more stress there is on each individual valve. And the number of valves could very well be determined by heredity, too.

PREGNANCY PLAYS A MAJOR ROLE IN DEVELOPING VARICOSE VEINS

Of all the topics touched upon so far, pregnancy, either current or past, is probably the biggest single factor in causing (and accelerating) the development of varicose veins in women. The reasons are complex and varied. There are several factors that probably all contribute.

1. A pregnant woman has more blood in her circulatory system. When you become pregnant, your body increases its blood volume in order to nourish the growing child. This increased blood supply (a pregnant woman has 20% more blood in her body than a similarly sized nonpregnant woman) is stored, to a large extent, in the venous system. Present thought is that the veins expand in order to hold this extra blood, and that it's this expansion that can lead to varicosities in women who are hereditarily predisposed.[6]

2. The growing uterus may have a profound effect, too. In both sexes, the main veins of the lower extremities pass up through the center of the legs, and through the pelvis. The pelvis is a large, butterfly-shaped bowl, whose upper edges are your hips; you can feel the high, thin bones through your skin. The lower edges of the bowl are the bones you sit on. There, the sockets of the upper leg bones attach.

In the soft tissues of the groin, the front of the bowl consists mostly of ligaments that connect the muscles of your legs to your abdomen. These ligaments protect a large opening in the pelvis at the top of each leg that serves as the passageway for the main artery and vein, as well as major nerves, lymphatic ducts, and so on.

The large bowl-shaped pelvis serves other functions besides that of anchoring your legs to your body. The pelvis supports the inner organs in its bowl-shaped form and to a large degree protects them from possible injury. In the pelvic girdle, as anatomists and physicians call the bowl, rest the bladder, the large and small intestines, and, above them in the abdomen, all the other major internal organs: liver, kidneys, spleen, gall bladder, pancreas, stomach.

Women, of course, have the uterus, fallopian tubes, and ovaries nestled within the pelvis, too. When pregnancy occurs, the uterus expands enough within nine months to compress all the organs that in times of nonpregnancy peacefully coexist with the uterus. Pregnant women in the last trimester often experience a need to urinate frequently; that's the effect of the enlarged uterus leaving very little room for the bladder.

A similar effect occurs with the major blood vessels passing nearby, carrying blood to and from the legs. As the uterus grows, pressure on the large veins grows, too, until at some point the flow of blood is impeded enough so that the blood system of the lower extremities backs up.

The effect of this slowdown is increased pressure downward in the veins in the legs. The venous action is always trying to send blood up, up to the heart. The back-pressure caused by compression by the uterus tends to reverse this action and turn it backward. Yet the venous system continues, by all the means at its disposal, to propel the blood forward. With these two forces in direct opposition, something's got to give.

The strain that results can cause stretching of the veins in the legs and damage to the tiny valves in those veins. These small, delicate structures, so useful in channeling and gently directing the blood's flow, are pressured from above as well as below. They can't swing both ways; they weren't designed to. At the site of the valves, the pressure from above is the greatest, and any of several things can occur.

The valves themselves can simply collapse and stop functioning. Blood flows both ways—this is the beginning of a varicose vein condition.

Or the valve can hold, and the vein itself can begin to stretch and distort. The vein can become wider at points where the pressure is the greatest and balloon out. The overall length of the vein can increase, too, causing the tortuous distortion that results in the snake-like appearance of a varicose vein.

A third possibility is the valve holds, and there's no visible damage. It may be years before the extra wear and tear makes itself evident as a varicose vein.

Or, of course, the fourth possibility. Nothing happens. This is one of the most puzzling things about varicose veins. Why do similar people with similar pregnancies not develop varicose vein problems in similar ways? Some women will be ravaged by varicose veins following a pregnancy, others will suffer moderately, slightly, or not at all. The arbitrary nature of the ailment leads us to believe that other factors, such as family history, missing genetic information, or missing membranes or proteins, hold some of the answers.

Pregnant patients may also experience varicosities, along with all the symptoms, in the vulval area, or also in the anus (hemorrhoids). As the pregnancy continues, these varicosities can get increasingly painful and uncomfortable. Some patients have reported that these vulval varicosities get worse with each succeeding pregnancy, but they usually subside between pregnancies.

3. Maybe hormones are to blame. While the extra blood in a pregnant woman's circulatory system or the growing uterus pressing against important blood vessels can cause varicose veins to form, the fact that some women start to develop varicose veins when they're only several **weeks** pregnant tells us there must be something else.

That something else involves the enormous changes a woman's body goes through as soon as the pregnancy begins.

As soon as conception occurs, a woman's body is flooded with hormones—hormones that trigger all the other vast changes her body will soon go through. It's these hormones (mostly estrogen and progesterone, among many others) that will keep the pregnancy going forward, and prepare the mother-to-be for delivery and lactation.

Because of increased estrogens and progesterone, blood vessels called shunts open in pregnant women. These act as shortcuts between the arteries and veins, helping to direct the flow of blood and move it faster. Sometimes these shunts are visible near the surface of the skin, where they appear as spider veins—commonly seen in the faces of pregnant women. They usually close after the pregnancy ends (and the hormone level drops), returning to their normal state of function.

Some researchers believe that if too many shunts open up, or if enough of them fail to close, they will add a stress to some parts of the venous system, and may play a role in the development of varicose veins.

But there are other theories as well. Estrogen and progesterone, the main hormones we've been talking about, aren't the only hormones that are produced during a pregnancy. Produced in much smaller amounts are substances that are critical for the later stages of pregnancy and the birth of the baby itself. As a pregnancy continues, the joints of the body must become more flexible, so that the head of the infant can pass through the pelvis. During delivery, the pelvis actually changes shape and flexes.

So the body produces a hormone (relaxin) that turns the hard cartilage and ligaments in the joints soft and rubbery, so that when the baby moves through the birth canal, the whole lower part of the mother's body stretches and expands.

Perhaps, in some women, this same substance has an effect on other tissues in the body, as well. This could cause stretching and distortion throughout the venous system, and throughout the various structures that help to support the veins, especially in the lower legs, where the pressures on the veins and valves are the greatest. When the veins stretch at the site of the valves, the valves can be pulled apart, and stop functioning.[7]

BIRTH CONTROL PILLS CAN ENCOURAGE VARICOSE VEINS, TOO

Oral contraceptives fool the body into thinking it's pregnant already by adding artificial hormones into the body's chemical system, and—like pregnancy—can be a contributing factor in the development of varicose veins. Again, the proof isn't in, but the evidence seems to point to that conclusion. Birth control pills have other effects on the venous system, in addition to many other organs. The pill increases the risk of blood clots in the venous system as well as thrombophlebitis. If you take birth control pills and you suspect you're developing varicose veins, you probably are.

OBESITY CAN BE AN IMPORTANT FACTOR IN THE DEVELOPMENT AND PROGRESS OF VARICOSITIES

As with many other things in life, the way your body's circulatory system functions depends to a large degree on how well you maintain it. Obesity and/or lack of exercise, poor muscle tone, or just immobility can all be important contributing factors, for pretty obvious reasons.

Obesity puts a strain on your body in many ways, so it's not too surprising that when your heart has to nourish many more—and bigger—cells than the average-sized person's heart must, the pressure on the blood vessels will be greater. A fat person's veins aren't any stronger than a thin person's, but they contain more blood.

A fat person's body has a lower proportion of muscle to body weight, and since the muscles are a critical part of the veins' pumping mechanism, the combination of greater blood volume and less muscle to support the veins in holding it and pumping it around is a dangerous one. The sheer weight of the blood, pulled toward the ground by the ever-present force of gravity, puts a significantly greater load on the walls of the veins of fat people, especially in the lower legs, than on those of thin people. The veins may stretch and distort, the valves may fail or leak, the blood may pool.

THE FASHION FACTOR

Although never proven, it is suspected that girdles, knee-high hose with snug elastic tops, control-top pantyhose, and other tight-fitting clothing or undergarments can harm circulation and add to the venous back-pressure that causes the system to clog. True, some doctors prescribe support hose to combat varicose veins, but those support garments support the whole leg **progressively**. A pair of pantyhose that's tighter at the elastic waistband than at the ankle will act like a roadblock to the traffic of blood moving back to the heart, perhaps aggravating or worsening a slowly developing condition. When you consider that many people wear these types of garments daily for years, you can see how serious an impact they can have. If you've got varicose veins, these garments could make them worse. If you don't have them yet, these garments could accelerate their development.

THE FLAB FACTOR

Without the help of the muscles, the veins don't work very well at all. If the muscles are flabby and weak, that doesn't help matters. A well-toned muscle can propel blood back to the heart by squeezing against the vein that runs nearby more efficiently than an untoned muscle. And the act of exercise itself helps charge up your circulatory system for the whole day or longer, benefits your heart and lungs, and keeps your circulatory system working better and more smoothly.

In fact, if you suffer from primary varicose veins, exercise may also bring about some measure of immediate relief, though probably not as much as raising your legs will. The action of your muscles will help to move the blood along its way, and the more vigorous the exercise is, the more it will help. (There is good evidence that by exercising frequently and regularly you can actually help your muscles take over some of the circulatory function that your veins can't handle. That's why you'll find a whole chapter on the subject of exercise further along in this book.)

THE FIBER FACTOR

You are what you eat, as the saying goes, and when it comes to the causes of varicose veins, there is evidence that what you eat influences how well your circulatory system works. The link may seem indirect, but it's not: Western diets tend to feature foods high in proteins, fats, and carbohydrates, but low in fiber. Our digestive systems need fiber to keep things functioning smoothly, and when that fiber is lacking, things tend to bog down. Constipation is the result, and there is a direct path connecting constipation to the development of varicose veins.

When people are constipated, and try to move their bowels, they tend to strain and push. It's the straining and pushing that can have a detrimental effect on the venous sytem by putting pressure on the large, thin-walled veins that pass near the large intestine through the pelvis. In much the same way that the expanding uterus in pregnant women is believed to obstruct these important veins, increasing the back-pressure along the entire lower circulatory system, constipation can, too. The pressure on the blood in the veins increases up and down the legs, forcing the vein walls to balloon out near the delicate valves, pulling them apart, enabling blood to seep back down the leg.

There's been a lot written about the importance of fiber in our diets, and a lot of that information has touched upon the serious diseases—colon cancer and diverticulitis, for instance—that may be avoided by simply eating more fiber every day. To that list we can perhaps add varicose veins, too.

In fact, the most common form of varicose veins is **directly** connected to not eating enough fiber. Hemorrhoids are really nothing but varicose veins that develop in the anus, caused by the stresses and strains of constipation. Here's a case where, by simply putting the digestive system back on tract, the condition will often resolve itself.

As for varicose veins elsewhere in the body, can merely eating more fiber prevent them? Probably not. But if you are hereditarily predisposed to varicose veins, there's a good chance that adding fiber to your diet, together with other commonsense precautions, could slow the process down.

There are so many theories as to why varicose veins appear. You may never know exactly what caused (or is causing) yours. That's why a cautious program of "preventive maintenance" is not a bad idea. Further on in this book you'll see that there are things you can actively do to counteract the forces that might be the cause of your varicosities.

CHAPTER 3

SYMPTOMS

HOW DO I KNOW IF I HAVE VARICOSE VEINS?

Most of the time, you just know.

If you've been feeling more and more self-conscious about the way you look at the beach or at the gym, or if you've wondered where all those bluish lines on your thighs and calves have come from, then the answer is fairly obvious. But what about those one or two odd-looking squiggles on your legs? Are they varicose veins? And, if they are, does that mean that more may develop? Are there warning signals you can rely on that can indicate that you should be seeking help now, before things get out of hand? And are there ways to tell if your varicose veins are indicative of a more serious condition?

Yes, there are. Varicose veins are so common that there are symptoms any sufferer will immediately recognize.

Varicose veins themselves are usually blue or purple, or sometimes bluish green, sometimes protruding out from the skin, but sometimes not. They're often accompanied by small clusters of spider veins, but not necessarily.

Varicose veins are often accompanied by swelling of the lower legs, sluggishness, and throbbing pains or bursting feelings that get worse at the end of the day. Typically, a varicose vein sufferer will describe achy feet, dull or stabbing pains in the legs, or burning or itching.

Of course, not all achy pains are varicose veins (they could be muscle pains, or strains or pulled tendons, bone pains or nerve problems). Nor is it unusual for people to suffer from swelling in the legs or feet (injuries or strains could cause that). Discolorations of the lower legs could be traced to bruises or some other injury. Throbbing or stabbing pains occur for other reasons, too. (Arthritis, joint problems, or pinched nerves spring to mind.) It's when all these signs occur together that varicose veins is a likely diagnosis.

How do you know if you have a tendency toward varicose veins? How do you know if you have any symptoms?

Let's ask some questions.

DOES ANYONE IN YOUR IMMEDIATE FAMILY HAVE VARICOSE VEINS?

If your mother, or someone closely related to you, has or has had varicose veins, you're at increased risk of getting them yourself. The more people in your immediate family that have or have had varicose veins, the greater your risk. Someone whose maternal grandmother has them, but whose mother does not, is not at as great a risk as someone whose maternal and paternal grandmother, father and mother, and two older sisters have them.

DO YOU EVER EXPERIENCE DISCOMFORT IN YOUR LEGS?

Many—but not all—varicose vein sufferers do experience some form of discomfort or pain, in varying degrees. Some people feel nothing. Perhaps your legs feel heavy, tired. Many patients complain of pressure in the legs, or a dull aching feeling, or night cramps—spasms that last for only a few seconds and disappear.

One 30-year-old patient said of her veins, "They feel like they quiver. Sometimes I think they feel like a worm under my skin. Other times, there's a dull pain, a tense feeling in the back of my knees. It's not very pleasant. I feel bad for other people when I see them with varicose veins. They look like how I feel."

Other people complain of burning, itching sensations, usually where the vein is most swollen and disfigured.

Some people experience pain that increases as the day wears on, pain that starts as dull pressure but can become sharp and stabbing, and can be relieved only by lying down and raising the legs.

It's very significant that many women notice more pain during their menstrual periods. Hormone levels in the blood have a direct bearing on varicose veins, and when these levels are high—like during your period— the level of discomfort is higher, too.

IF YOU FEEL PAIN OR DISCOMFORT, WHAT KIND OF DISCOMFORT DO YOU FEEL?

The kind of discomfort you may feel is an important clue to whether or not you have varicose veins. Generally, if a patient develops pains suddenly, it's more medically worrisome. It could be an indication that a problem has suddenly occurred inside an artery, not a vein, and the patient should seek medical attention immediately. More often, the varicose vein sufferer has been enduring aches and pains for a long period, and these may (or may not) increase in severity gradually with the passing of time. (Of course, not all chronic or long-term pains need be due to veins, as we said. If you experience chronic pains, see a doctor.)

WHEN DO YOU FEEL DISCOMFORT? If you suspect you have varicose veins, **when** you feel pain is nearly as important as the kind of pain you have. The classic varicose vein sufferer will feel worse as the day goes on, as fluids collect in the lower extremeties. An ex-waitress said, "At the end of a long day on my feet, my legs were just one big dull ache." (So uncomfortable was her condition that she changed careers.) This is typical. People who spend the day standing or sitting are affected by the force of gravity, and the longer they don't move around, the more fluids settle to their bodies' lowest point. It's even worse on warm days, as the body tries to cool itself off by naturally dilating the veins closest to the surface of the skin. The body's inability to efficiently move those fluids back to the heart can cause swelling of the ankles and lower legs, in some cases. Sometimes, the ankles and feet will become so swollen that the skin dimples, what doctors call pitted edema. ("Edema" is the medical term for soft, tender swelling caused by excess fluids in the tissues.)

If you spend your day in the same spot, if you have a desk job or an occupation that keeps you on your feet all day (like a barber, a dental hygienist, a bank teller, or any of dozens of other vocations that keep us from walking or moving frequently) and you feel a heaviness or hard-to-describe sensation of pressure, this could be a sign of developing varicose veins. Try pressing your thumb into your calf at the end of a typical day. If you can make a dimple in your skin that doesn't disappear for several minutes, consider that to be another warning signal. That'll tip you off to possible fluid retention, and perhaps an insufficiency in your venous system's ability to return blood to the deep system.

WHAT MAKES IT FEEL BETTER? What makes it feel better is also a good indication of whether or not you may have varicosities. When you relax in the evening or after a day at work, try elevating your legs. In the average varicose vein sufferer, raising your legs above your heart will allow the blood and other fluids in your legs to make their way to your heart with the help of gravity. The pain and heavy, bloated feeling in your legs should fade. The same principle is at work after a good night's sleep; many varicose vein sufferers will feel great, because their horizontal position while asleep makes their circulatory system's job easier.

If you suffer from what you think are varicose veins, and elevating your legs does not relieve the pain, alert your doctor. The presence of pain could indicate arterial insufficiency, muscle or bone problems, arthritis, back trouble, or nerve damage. A thorough physical exam will help your doctor to pinpoint the problem.

WHERE ARE YOUR SUSPECTED VARICOSE VEINS? The location of your symptoms is a good indication as to whether or not you have varicose veins. The architecture of the human body is surprisingly consistent; that is, everybody usually has the same veins running in the same areas, with slight variations. So varicose veins tend to trace the routes of the major superficial veins. See the diagram in the Anatomy and Physiology chapter and you'll see the path of the major superficial vein—the long saphenous vein—and its major branches, including the lesser saphenous vein in the calf area. These two veins, and their tributaries, are the most common sites for varicose veins.

Varicose veins are most common in the lower legs below the knee, though quite a few people have them above the knee, too. Very rarely do true varicose veins occur above the waist, even though spider veins are found nearly everywhere, but usually on the face and thighs.

DO YOU OFTEN HAVE SWELLING IN YOUR LOWER LEGS OR ANKLES? When the circulatory system is not functioning efficiently, it's difficult for it to remove the fluids that collect in the tissues. This is especially true in the lower extremities, again because the effect of gravity tends to pull fluids into the lower parts of the body. With little help from the other circulatory forces in the body to collect these fluids and return them to the heart, the fluids stay, filling the tissues. The result is edema, a soft swelling in the ankles and feet that may be accompanied by a flushed color, or perhaps skin rashes.

Edema can lead to a set of symptoms that are very characteristic of advanced varicose veins. The tissues in the lower leg become chronically swollen—the swelling doesn't go away. The presence of excess fluids can then disrupt the delicately balanced capillary action that nourishes and cleanses the tissues on a cellular level.

This causes the skin to change, and decrease its barrier function to bacteria. The area is likely to be painful, tender to the touch. The skin can become brittle and red, thin and fragile, and susceptible to cuts or tears.

When that happens, skin rashes and infections, called eczema and dermatitis result. Sometimes these infections can progress to the tissues underneath. This causes a condition called cellulitis.

Consequently, when things have progressed this far, other symptoms can appear too. In localized areas, the capillaries can begin to leak red blood cells under the skin, leaving a brown stain called *pigmentation* (the blood cells themselves are re-absorbed; the brown color is from iron in the blood that stays behind).

If this condition is left untreated, it will eventually get worse as the cells begin to break down and die. The result is an *ulcer*, a large, unsightly sore that will heal very slowly or not at all, depending on the condition of the surrounding tissue. When the circulation of an area breaks down to such a degree that ulceration occurs, the healing process is seriously impaired; the living cells in that area are simply not being nourished, their wastes are not being collected, and they are dying. *Ulcers are a serious medical problem that must be treated by a doctor.* See the next chapter, Complications, for a more detailed discussion of these advanced symptoms of varicose veins.

DO YOU EVER BLEED FROM YOUR VEINS? Sometimes varicose veins bleed spontaneously, usually in people who have had varicosities for a long time. Bleeding varicose veins are a serious signal that medical treatment is necessary, and needed immediately. Bleeding varicosities heal slowly, and, if the vein is a large one, substantial blood loss could occur. It's very rare, but if significant bleeding occurs when the patient is unaware of it, such as at night during sleep, death can result. So, while bleeding to death from varicose veins is not an everyday occurrence, it can happen.

Now that you know many of the ways that varicose veins can occur, and how to recognize them as they are occurring, you can learn the more hopeful aspects of this condition: treatment and cure.

CHAPTER 4

WHEN VARICOSE VEINS ARE DANGEROUS

COMPLICATIONS

Varicose veins, as we've said, are rarely medically significant. Even though they might be ugly, they are rarely dangerous. And if you take the simplest steps, chances are they won't have any significant effect on your general health.

But "rarely" medically significant doesn't mean "never." For instance, ignoring a case of varicose veins for years and years can lead to serious complications, some of which could ultimately, although rarely, be life-threatening. And there are other times when what may appear to the layman to be a case of common varicose veins is really an indication of a far more serious problem that your doctor should know about immediately.

COMMON VARICOSE VEINS VS. UNCOMMON VARICOSE VEINS

If you think you have varicose veins, chances are overwhelming that you do. And that's all. Of the patients who come in for treatment 99.9% have no symptoms or diseases other than this. These run-of-the-mill varicose veins are known as **primary varicose veins** because the patient's condition has no known origin in any other disease. The complaint—the primary complaint—is the obvious visible symptom: the veins themselves.

Far more rare are varicose veins that form because other systems in the body are not functioning properly due to disease, traumatic injury, or other abnormalities. When another condition causes varicose veins, they are known as **secondary varicose veins**, because the primary complaint is any of several underlying causes. Usually, these underlying causes are fairly serious, indicating a substantial disruption of the circulatory system. But, as we've said, these conditions are quite rare and are usually easily diagnosed by a qualified physician. So don't jump to conclusions that your own ailment means you are grievously ill. Further on in this chapter will be other accompanying symptoms of secondary varicose veins.

COMPLICATIONS: WHAT CAN HAPPEN IF PRIMARY VARICOSE VEINS GO UNTREATED

Varicose veins are a form of venous insufficiency. This simply means that the veins in the affected area are not efficiently moving blood and other fluids away from the cells and up into the rest of the circulatory system.

Mild venous insufficiency is not by itself a serious medical problem. But moderate to severe venous insufficiency is cause for concern, and severe insufficiency can lead to serious complications.

EDEMA

The first of these complications is a chronic swelling known as edema, usually appearing in the area of the ankle. It may be transitory at first, but edema is capable of becoming a chronic condition. The swollen area can be tender to the touch, or itch. Edema is the collection of fluids in the tissues that won't reenter the general circulatory system, because the basic forces that drive the circulatory system at the cellular level are disturbed.

At the level of the capillaries, where the width of each vessel is microscopic, the driving force that pushes— and pulls fluids from the capillaries into the tissues and back again—is a subtle, finely balanced mechanism of many forces. As long as the pressures are in equilibrium, fluids and nutrients travel easily from the arterial capillaries to the cells and then back into the venous capillaries and onward.

Many things can cause these equilibriums between the circulatory system and the tissues to change. An injury, like a bump on the head, or your body's allergic reaction to a foreign substance can cause a shift in the comparative pressures within the circulatory system. That's why you swell up—the bump on the head results in a "goose egg," a localized imbalance, and the allergic reaction can cause a systemic change in pressure at the capillary level, so you swell up all over.

Varicose veins can cause the equilibrium to change, too. When the blood isn't moving smoothly farther downstream in the system, because of faulty valves and distended, inefficient veins, everything can slow down enough to cause a significant increase in backward pressure that can be felt down to the capillary level.

It's not an immediate effect of varicose veins, to be sure. It may take years for this swelling to develop. But once these changes take place, the swelling will become long-term, and will respond only temporarily to the usual remedies for lower leg swelling, such as raising the legs or wearing support stockings.

STASIS

Long-term edema is a form of **stasis**. The term "stasis" refers to the stagnation of the fluids in the tissues, and it's this stagnation that causes subsequent damage to the skin. The skin will become very tender and fragile as it loses its elasticity and its ability to "bounce back" from injury. It will tend to tear and cut easily, and heal slowly. In some places the tissues get hard and thick, while in others they seem stretched too thin.

Angry red rashes can occur, known as **stasis dermatitis**, that itch and, eventually, "weep"—ooze a clear fluid that seems to have no specific source. Characteristically, it will heal on its own, only to return, then heal again—a cycle that will be repeated many times. Each time the dermatitis returns, the skin pays a price of lost elasticity and ability to heal.

As the condition gets worse, the actual fabric of the skin starts to break down, and as it does, the tissue's protective barrier against infection breaks down, too.

ULCERS

Ulcers are the eventual result. When the skin can no longer fight off infection and can no longer heal on its own, small, constantly draining sores appear in the affected areas. They will heal only very slowly (sometimes over a period of a year or more) or not at all. The sores may grow ever larger, merging into large, ugly, dangerous infected areas covering the lower legs.

When ulcers occur, it is necessary to see a physician immediately. An ulcer is the end result of serious, neglected venous insufficiency, and is a severe medical emergency for several reasons. The body's first line of defense—the skin—is breached and open to infection. Once established, an infection can spread throughout the body, causing serious, even life-threatening, problems.

Ulcers will also recur again and again, unless their root causes are treated. Each time they return, the ulcers will heal more and more slowly, and a doctor will have to take more and more heroic measures to help them. First there will be bandages, then support bandages, then a kind of stiff, medicated bandage in the shape of a boot that the patient will have to wear for an extended period of time. Surgery may be needed, and skin grafts are also a possibility.

Ulcers only occur in the last stages of a long-term varicose vein condition that has been ignored for many years. It's important to watch for any unusual changes in your skin, as these may be a precursor to a serious stasis-related condition. Obese people are especially prone to stasis problems and should be especially wary. Monitor yourself closely. If you suspect you suffer from edema or stasis dermatitis, see your doctor.

VARICOSE VEINS CAN BECOME INFLAMED

About 5% of well-established varicose veins are liable to develop a condition called **superficial thrombophlebitis**. ''Thrombo'' means blood clot, ''phlebitis'' means inflammation. Put them together and you are describing an inflammation of the vein, accompanied by a blood clot inside the vessel. Sometimes the inflammation comes first, and causes the clot; sometimes the blood clot causes the inflammation. (''Superficial'' refers to the vein's location within the circulatory system; further on in this chapter we'll talk briefly about deep-system thrombophlebitis, a more serious condition.)

If a doctor is alerted to the condition, it's not likely to be a cause for worry. Ninety-nine percent of all cases of superficial thrombophlebitis are easily treated.

Three things contribute to the formation of blood clots:
1) The slowing down of the circulation
2) Injury to the inner lining of the vein wall
3) A thickening of the blood

Two of these are common to varicose veins, and occasionally cause blood clots. This is what is called superficial phlebitis.

The resulting condition appears as a tender red cord over the inflamed vein that can extend all the way up the leg. It can start as the result of minor injury to the vein.

Treatment is usually a local one. Hot packs are applied to the area, and the patient is often given aspirin or some mild anti-inflammatory drug. Perhaps an anticoagulating drug, which will prevent further clotting action, will be prescribed, too. Support hose, applied to the area, and some walking are also indicated, as these will help restore the circulation in the area, prevent further clotting action, and help the vein to heal itself. Superficial thrombophlebitis does not have any significance other than its discomfort, because the blood clots do not travel elsewhere. Note that superficial thrombophlebitis is different than deep vein thrombophlebitis which has nothing to do with varicose veins.

SECONDARY VARICOSITIES: WHEN VARICOSE VEINS MEAN SOMETHING ELSE

We've just seen that there are several conditions associated with advanced, or long-ignored, varicose vein problems. These conditions stem from the fact that the superficial circulatory system is operating inefficiently, and that inefficiency can be traced back to the failure of certain major superficial veins in the legs.

But there are times when varicose veins are a symptom of something else. There are several major problems of the deep circulatory system or other diseases and congenital malformations that do cause varicose veins. They are comparatively rare, though—so think twice before rushing out to the emergency room—and they are almost always accompanied by other distinctive symptoms that would tip off your doctor that there is something besides ordinary varicose veins at work.

THE EFFECTS AND AFTEREFFECTS OF DEEP-SYSTEM THROMBOPHLEBITIS

The superficial venous system feeds directly into the deep venous system, major large veins that run far below the surface. Deep-system thrombophlebitis is an inflammation caused by a blood clot in one of these deep-system veins, and it's a serious problem with several life-threatening implications.

Former President Richard Nixon suffered from bouts of phlebitis, and the disease got much attention precisely because it is so potentially debilitating. Blood clots, forming suddenly or over a period of time, can break off and travel to the heart and lungs.

The blood clot, once established in the deep-system vein, is on a direct line to the heart and lungs. If part of the clot should break free it would be propelled straight to the heart, and then to the lungs, where it could be fatal. The blood clot blocks part of the blood flow to the lungs. This can cause the oxygen level to drop dangerously. In addition, sudden heart failure can result from the greatly increased resistance to the flow of blood from the heart to the lungs, due to the blockage. This is called an **embolism.**

This dangerous potential event is what differentiates ordinary superficial thrombophlebitis from deep-vein thrombophlebitis.

The symptoms of deep-vein thrombophlebitis appear locally, in the leg. Pain, swelling, and tenderness of the leg reflect the slowing of the deep vein's blood flow. Depending on where the clot is, these symptoms can occur in just part of the leg, or can involve the entire leg.

These attacks of deep-vein thrombophlebitis can be dramatic events, requiring special medical attention. The patient is immediately hospitalized and put on a program of strong anticoagulants to dissolve the clots and prevent the formation of new ones, and to prevent embolism. Treatment is likely to be long-term, with the situation carefully monitored.

The after effects of deep-system thrombophlebitis can involve permanent damage to the deep vein or its valves. This is the cause of **post-phlebitic syndrome**. One of post-phlebitic syndrome's symptoms is varicose veins, and the associated symptoms that go along with them. With no valves to help the deep-system vein move blood up to the heart, pressure falls back onto the superficial veins, which, in much the same way as happens with primary varicose veins, causes a chain reaction of valve failures throughout the leg. Sometimes the superficial veins take over the function of the deep veins because the deep veins are so badly damaged.

Varicose veins caused by post-phlebitic syndrome, however, tend to be accompanied by more severe symptoms of venous insufficiency—edema, stasis, dermatitis, the possibility of ulceration and under-the-skin pigmentation—reflecting the problems of the deep-system.

Sadly, there is no known treatment for the underlying cause of post-phlebitic syndrome except certain conservative measures. Individual symptoms are treated

locally when they flare up, but there is no effective way
at the moment to repair the valve damage in the deep-
system vein. Some experimentation is being done with
valve transplants, but the surgery involved is very tricky
and, as yet, unproven.

OTHER CIRCULATORY BLOCKAGES

Far more rare than even phlebitis or post-phlebitic
syndrome are other blockages that can appear in or near
major blood vessels, causing the flow of blood to stop
enough so that superficial veins become varicose. Again,
these blockages are usually accompanied by other symptoms, such as sharp pains, or visible abnormalities, like
swellings, or differences in the sizes of limbs.

Sometimes an injury, tumor, or growth of scar tissue located in the leg, pelvis, or abdomen can cause the
free flow of blood to and from the lower circulatory
system to be interrupted. The location of the blockage
will determine where the varicosities occur. They could
be anywhere, even in places where varicose veins almost never "normally" appear.

Should your doctor suspect a blockage of this sort,
he or she will look for tender or painful areas that seem
to lead to the visible varicosities. Since a blockage or
tumor can affect either the arterial or venous system, a
venograph and an arteriograph—tests that show the
flow of blood—would be required. As serious as these
situations can be, diagnoses of circulatory blockages are
fairly simple. In such a case, the more difficult question
will be determining what caused the blockage in the
first place, and how to restore the circulation.

SPECIAL CASES OF VARICOSE VEINS

There is a group of varicose veins that are not caused by a disease as such, but rather by very specific congenital problems that have more to do with an abnormal way the body developed from conception.

In some extremely rare cases, the circulatory system develops without any valves, or with important parts missing. There are cases where the arteries and veins have unusual connections called *fistulas*, so that the blood travels directly from one to the other, bypassing the capillaries.

In nearly all of these conditions, the appearance of varicose veins will coincide with other abnormal symptoms.

KLIPPEL-TRENAUNAY SYNDROME

Varicose veins are extremely rare in people under the age of 25, except in women who have had several children. When varicose veins are seen in children, one reason is the rare congenital condition Klippel-Trenaunay Syndrome, characterized by an abnormal "architecture" of the deep venous system.

Klippel-Trenaunay children often have distinctive birthmarks, such as port-wine stain. Their limbs can be of different sizes, too.

ARTERIOVENOUS FISTULA

This basic malformation of the circulatory system, with its abnormal connections from the arterial to venous system and disproportionate blood flow to various parts of the body, can result in the appearance of varicose veins, often on only one side of the body.

Fistula is the medical term for connection, and an arteriovenous fistula (AV fistula) is a serious birth defect that channels blood from one system directly into the other, without going into the capillaries.

As we'll discuss in the next chapter, Spider Veins, the circulatory system does include numerous "shunts" between the arterioles (tiny arteries) and venules to regulate the rate of blood flow to the capillaries, the pressure of that flow, and where the blood is directed. AV fistula, by contrast, involves major blood vessels instead of the shunts, and the flow of arterial blood directly into the veins (or vice versa) can be substantial, causing the veins to distend and distort from the high pressure of the arterial blood. AV fistula is a rare, unusual birth defect, and one that can only be corrected (if at all) with surgery to reconnect the system correctly.

Varicose veins need not be a serious, life-threatening disorder. Chances are slim you will ever have reason to think they could be. But if you suspect that your condition is at all unusual in any respect, seek prompt medical attention. This book does not profess to teach you to diagnose and treat yourself; that's what a doctor is for. Even if your condition seems "typical," confirm this with a qualified physician. Do not take unnecessary risks with your health.

CHAPTER 5

SPIDER VEINS

WHAT ARE SPIDER VEINS?

Varicose veins, as we've explained them up to now, are the large, ugly, tortuous, and dilated blood vessels that fill up with blood due to valve failure. But these bulging, knotty vessels are not the only kind of cosmetic vein problem that drives people to seek treatment, and they're not the only vein problem that can be effectively treated—thanks to recent advances and careful medical techniques.

Sometimes smaller blood vessels, either blue or purple or red, appear gradually on the legs, the ankles, the upper thighs, or the face. Sometimes they'll appear elsewhere, too, like on the upper arms or the neck. Except for some that show up in women who are pregnant, they almost never disappear by themselves. They rarely exhibit any other symptom besides their unsightliness, though sometimes they might itch a little, or be mildly tender.

These are **"spider" veins**, so-called because they appear as a weblike, spidery netting—though they go by other names as well. Some people call them broken blood vessels or broken capillaries, but those misnomers speak mostly of people's misunderstanding of them. Doctors call spider veins by their formal name, telangiectases (tel-an-jē-ek′-tə-sez), and much the same way they divide the major varicose veins into categories, spiders can be classified as either primary or secondary. Primary spider veins are those that appear for no apparent reason, and with no other associated symptoms. Secondary spider veins are signs of other problems or diseases, some of which are quite serious (traumatic injury, liver disease, lupus erythematosus, exposure to radiation, excessive sunlight, or other carcinogens, for example). But secondary spider veins are quite rare.

Spider veins are so common that they are indeed Everyman's (or Everywoman's) disease. It's estimated that two thirds of all pregnant women develop them (though most due to pregnancy usually disappear about six weeks after delivery) and many men suffer, as well. Even children get spider veins.

Spider veins and varicose veins seem often to go together. Eighty percent of varicose vein sufferers will also have some spider veins, probably because the two conditions have similar causes. Fifty percent of spider vein sufferers also have some form of varicose veins, too.

WHAT DO THEY LOOK LIKE?

It's hard to mistake a spider vein. It looks like a red or blue or sometimes purplish thread right at the surface of the skin. Maybe you'll only have a single spider, but they more often appear in groups, and they generally crop up in some very particular areas.

The outside of the thigh or the back of the knee, for instance, or the inside of the ankle. Or on the face, the area flanking the nose, or the nose itself, especially near the nostrils.

Spider veins, while generally tiny, can vary in size from .5 mm to 2 to 3 mm in diameter, and can be any variety of lengths or configurations. Some are so small they can hardly be seen as individual blood vessels at all. Others are larger, appearing as blue or red or somewhere in between, as thick as a human hair or a thread. These often have no apparent beginning or end, and no rhyme or reason to their placement on a leg or thigh. They just appear.

Spiders characteristically form tiny networks. Several will link up in a clear vein pattern. Others will be so tiny that the network appears as just a pink spot that won't go away; under a little magnification, though, the spider web form becomes apparent.

Usually, they don't hurt. They rarely bleed. Except for the slight itchiness some of them bring, or subtle changes in the skin texture in the affected areas, they are generally without symptoms. They can't be predicted, and they probably cannot be prevented in people who have a predisposition for them. But they can be treated.

The difference between spider veins and their larger cousins, varicose veins, is more than just size. Spider veins, whether they are arterial, venous, or something in-between (their exact nature is a subject of some disagreement among doctors), are vessels without the tiny valves that are so important to true varicosities. What they are is dilated capillaries. Why they are dilated is still unclear. Because spider veins often crop up at pregnancy, or after a patient has been taking birth control pills, some researchers believe that estrogens and the little arterio-venous shunts are the cause, though the link is more implied than proven.

THE ROLE OF THE SHUNTS

The fresh blood that goes to the cells passes from large arteries to much smaller and smaller ones, until it reaches the capillary level. But if the system was as simple as that, every capillary and every cell would receive exactly the same amount of oxygen and nutrients as every other cell.

That isn't what happens, however. When specific parts of your body need extra energy for specific tasks, like your legs while jogging or your brain while thinking, a fantastically complex mechanism directs the blood, closing some parts of the system down a little, opening other parts up, calling for reserves from the venous system where the extra blood is stored.

An important part of that mechanism is the tiny shunts that act as bypasses around the capillaries throughout the body. These shunts, upon command, will all act in unison toward the common goal of sending more blood where it's needed.

Say you're walking through the snow. Your leg muscles need more energy at that moment than your other organs do, so the blood flow will be directed to your muscles in general, and your leg muscles in particular. At the same time, in your thigh muscles, the arteries and veins will dilate and work in conjunction with the shunts to increase the blood flow to the cells that are working hard to take each step.

A spider vein seems to happen when shunts like these occasionally get stuck in the ''open'' position.

Strangely, it doesn't happen all over the body, just in the specific areas where spiders usually appear. Why this is, is unknown.

The spider occurs just slightly downstream from the opened shunt. The pressure of extra blood constantly flowing into this small venule directly from an arteriole is enough to dilate it, filling it with blood and giving it that distinctive deep color that is easily visible through the skin.

But what causes the shunts to open? We have a good idea that estrogen plays a role. When a woman becomes pregnant, large quantities of this powerful hormone are produced in the body. One of the many functions of these hormones may be to increase blood flow to growing organs, by opening the shunt mechanism, and directing it to the uterus, for use by the growing fetus. Spider veins are a side effect of this action, and that explains why they occur so frequently in pregnant women.

There is one school of thought that says that spider veins can be either veins or arteries, and that the color of the vein indicates one or the other—bright red for arterial blood, blue for venous blood. From our experience, 99% of all spiders are venous, but it probably doesn't make any difference to the patient: treatment is the same, regardless.

SECONDARY SPIDERS: WHAT THEY COULD MEAN

As with varicose veins, the vast majority of people who suffer from spider veins have nothing wrong with them other than spider veins. But, rarely, there are some other conditions that show themselves with spiders, as well as numerous other symptoms.

SPIDER VEINS ARE A COMMON INDICATION OF ADVANCED LIVER DISEASE. While it's not too often that people coming to a doctor complaining of spider veins actually have liver disease, doctors do keep an eye out for the symptom because it is such a good indicator of liver problems. The reason again has to do with estrogens. The liver's function in the body is rather like that of a large and very efficient filter. Among the many things it removes—even in men—are estrogens, present in small amounts. When there is liver disease, such as in **cirrhosis**, this filtrating action is diminished, the estrogen level in the body increases.

Look at the facial features of alcoholics, who have destroyed their liver's function, and you'll see evidence of these high levels of unfiltered estrogens. Spider veins, often on the cheeks, nose, or neck, are characteristic of late-stage alcoholism precisely because of this principle, coupled with the tendency of alcohol to make the skin flush. After many years of drinking, the flush becomes permanent.

Spider veins in liver disease, though, are markedly different from the type associated with varicose veins. They are more likely to appear other places on the body, like the chest and arms, and they generally appear redder, because they are more arterial in nature.

CAN SPIDER VEINS BE TREATED?

Absolutely. Over the years, doctors have tried to treat spiders, with varying success. In the past, only the wealthy could afford to have the condition treated. Covering makeups were tried, as were various electrodesiccation and fulgaration techniques (we'll explain those soon), but the results were often hit-and-miss.

However, today new procedures and a sophistication of techniques have made it possible virtually to eliminate (or, at least, greatly improve) even the most advanced spider vein conditions.

Before the latest innovations, the treatments mostly used were often more disfiguring than the spiders themselves, and except for a fairly narrow range of veins, simply not worth the trouble, or risk. Often, the patient merely traded the spider for a scar.

Electrocautery and **diathermy**, two similar techniques employing an electric current that runs through a small probe or blade, were used to "zap" the visible vein. If the vein was the right size—not too big, not too small—and the practitioner had a steady hand, a good result could be achieved. The current passed through the tissues the physician wanted to eliminate, coagulating the blood and disintegrating the living cells. The technique is still practiced today, especially for the elimination of small warts, moles, etc. **Fulgaration** and **electrodesiccation** (literally, "drying by electricity") are similar techniques, differing not in principle, but only in the type of method used to apply the electric current to the skin. These techniques may leave a small scar where the spider vein was, because that's how the vein is eliminated: the vein is "scarred down" to an almost invisible thread that, in theory, blends into the surrounding tissue.

These procedures are sometimes moderately effective. Problems arise when the area to be eliminated is larger than just a small spot. Then these tiny scars can become obvious.

The doctor's skill is the most important single aspect of the treatment. Needless to say, a slip of the probe will destroy healthy tissue wherever it finds it; the instrument cannot distinguish on its own what goes and what stays.

MODERN TECHNIQUES: THE ARGON LASER

A significant improvement over older electrodesiccation techniques is the argon laser, a hand-held instrument that can focus high energy on a tiny area. Perfectly suited to small spiders, less than ½ mm, the laser has the ability to shoot right through normal, healthy tissue, and eliminate only the spider vein. The result is a much more accurate, focusable treatment, with less scarring. Sometimes, however, the laser will leave a tiny light colored spot.

It takes about two months after treatment for the healing process to be complete.

SCLEROTHERAPY

Also called injection therapy, sclerotherapy is one of the oldest varicose vein procedures. New refinements to this old technique, including very fine needles, and milder, more predictable solutions mean that the range of spiders that can be treated now extends to the very small.

Sclerotherapy works by injecting a sclerosing solution, a compound that irritates the inner lining of the spider. The vein dries up and disappears from sight. Because the solution travels through the vein, it's easy to eliminate a whole network of interconnected spider veins with just one injection. The tissues near the vein are not affected. So sclerotherapy is especially well suited to treating extensive areas.

You can read more about both laser and sclerotherapy techniques further on in this book.

Spider veins are more an unattractive nuisance than a serious health threat, and they're so common that almost everyone is affected by them. There may have been a time when they were considered too trivial to do anything about, but that's no longer true, thanks to the ease and good results modern treatment techniques offer.

PART II

TREATMENT

CHAPTER 6

HOW ARE VARICOSE VEINS TREATED?

We thought you'd never ask.

Now that you know something about your body's blood system, and about the underlying causes of varicose veins, you can better understand how treatment can work.

The treatment of varicose veins and spider veins varies with the extent of the condition and the severity of each of the individual varicosities. It varies, too, with individual doctors, some of whom may be more familiar with one treatment method than another. And it also varies with the patient's expectation of what might be done and what the results could be.

Patients with little knowledge of the spectrum of available treatments may be letting themselves in for surprise or disappointment. If you didn't know that cars came with air-conditioning, you might be annoyed when you noticed everyone else on the highway sitting in cool comfort with their windows rolled up. The same thing is true with treatment for varicose veins. Many options exist, with varied results. Some of the most successful treatments are not well known, while some of the best-known are not necessarily the most successful. As with so many other things in life, when you become a consumer of varicose vein treatments, it pays to be an informed consumer. Making an informed choice will help you get what you're expecting.

The happy truth is that now there's so much that can be done to eliminate the symptoms, alleviate the unsightliness, and restore the circulatory system to its proper level of functioning.

Recent medical breakthroughs, new technologies, and sophisticated refinements in the areas of laser technology, microsurgery, chemistry, and ambulatory outpatient surgical techniques have made varicose veins easier to treat, with more pleasing results—both physiologically and cosmetically—than ever before. And new knowledge and understanding about the importance of diet, exercise, and good living habits can be put to good effect to help delay the onset of varicose veins, lessening their severity, and preventing complications.

Treatment falls into two basic areas. One school of thought is to give help to the damaged vein so it functions better. These techniques may attend to the physiological needs of the circulatory system, and may help slow down the development of new varicose veins, but for existing varicosities that mar the beauty of the patient's legs, they are generally not helpful. Once a vein has become "tortuous and dilated," in the words of the vascular surgeon, there is no known way to return it to its former state. The best these functional aids can do is to combat the forces that are causing the vein to distort, fight the further deterioration of the vein and valves, and try to restore the original circulatory patterns as much as possible. This is called conservative treatment.

The other philosophy is one of more aggressive

treatment. Here the goal of the physician is to take the affected vein out of service altogether, actually curing the condition by removing the malfunctioning veins. The blood is then rerouted to flow through other veins in the same area. The advantages to these techniques are many, but the most appealing to the sufferer of disfiguring varicose veins or spider veins (or, like most patients, of both) is the fact that after a successful program of treatment, no signs of the malfunctioning veins exist. They are simply gone. They won't come back. And with careful management and monitoring, new occurrences can be controlled before they cause any further problems.

1. CONSERVATIVE TREATMENTS: WHO ARE THEY FOR?

Conservative treatment is not a cure, but only a stopgap measure. It will somewhat prevent the condition from getting worse, and it will alleviate some of the more bothersome symptoms, such as the swelling, the aching, and the cramps.

As such, conservative treatments are not for everyone. Most people want to see their problem fixed and go away. But there are some patients for whom conservative treatments are the best option, or at least a valuable one.

People in ill health. Because of frail health, or advanced age, or both, some patients cannot afford even the minor risks that other varicose vein treatments entail. People with serious heart trouble, or other grievous illnesses, are often not strong enough to undergo surgery, or occasionally cannot even tolerate the medications used in sclerotherapy.

Pregnant women who can't take certain medications because of potential harm to their babies.

Patients who can't tolerate more aggressive procedures for other reasons, such as fear, economic considerations, or the inconvenience of undergoing other treatments.

WHAT ARE THE CONSERVATIVE TREATMENTS?

SUPPORT STOCKINGS

Probably the best known, and least favorite—among patients, anyway—of the functional aids for varicose veins, these are not the commonly available support hose that one can find in a department store—those wouldn't be effective. When a doctor recommends support stockings for a patient with varicose veins, he or she means prescription support stockings. The principle behind them is simple: Varicose veins are veins that fill up with blood, and are then unable to empty themselves of blood. Support hose work by keeping the varicose veins from filling up with blood in the first place.

Patients are generally instructed to keep their stockings near the bed, so that when they wake up in the morning, they can reach over—before getting up and inadvertently allowing the veins in their legs to fill with blood and start to swell—and put on the hose. The stockings are usually made out of a thick, sturdy elastic material (not the kind of garment you'd feel glamorous in at a cocktail party) and are not often available in any other color than beige (though some manufacturers are now marketing blacks and whites, as well). This type of stocking varies in pressure from ankle upward, the greatest pressure being at the ankle, with a gradual lessening of pressure the higher up the leg they go. The pressure of these garments is rated in millimeters (mm) of mercury (Hg), similar to the way the weather reporter describes atmospheric pressure. The higher the number, the greater the pressure. A heavy support stocking might be rated at 25 mm/Hg at the ankle, gradually lessening at the knee and thigh. The stockings must be carefully fitted to your leg, as a pair that's too loose or too tight either won't work or could actually be harmful in some cases.

When properly applied, by turning the stocking inside out, starting at the toe, then unrolling it up the leg as you go, the elastic pressure squeezes the large, dilated veins just under the surface of the legs, and closes them to any flow of blood. The constant pressure on the leg keeps fluids from pooling at the feet, and by doing this, should prevent the pain and discomfort usually associated with varicose veins at the end of a long day.

Some of the support stockings are elastic in two directions, some only one. While the fabrics are not sheer, some manufacturers show a little more sensitivity to the appearance of the wearer than others. To give you an idea of just how thick and heavy these support stockings tend to be, some doctors say that a pair lasts for **only** about six months. Ordinary panty hose are doing pretty well if they last six days.

The stockings come in various lengths, depending on the location of the varicose veins in the leg. Knee-highs, thigh lengths, and lengths that go to the waist are all available, as well as panty hose styles. They have to be carefully washed, or the elastic can wear out. And they're expensive. (The Products You Might Find Helpful appendix in the Resources section lists several manufacturers of support hose.)

But do they work? Somewhat. In the sense that they can prevent further deterioration of a varicose vein condition, they may be effective, at least in the short run. For relieving pain and discomfort from varicosities, especially if you must be on your feet all day, certainly they work. However, you're trading the discomfort of varicose vein problems for the discomfort of wearing these stockings, which in warm weather can be substantial. And you're trading the unsightliness of varicose veins for the unsightliness of thick, elastic hose. The underlying causes of varicosities remain, as do the varicosities that made you seek treatment in the first place.

Support hose are usually used when the patient, for whatever reason, won't be treated any other way. They're also useful as an adjunct to other ongoing therapy, and in cases where nothing else would be effective, such as in cases of post-phlebitic syndrome.

ACE BANDAGES

Some physicians use Ace bandages for the same reasons they might use support hose, though Ace bandages are a more inconvenient and temporary functional aid. Ace bandages used by themselves are not terribly satisfactory for the simple reason that they're difficult to properly apply, and when you walk around, they often slip, making it necessary to reapply them. They're wrapped around the entire foot, leaving the toes exposed, and then spiral-wrapped up the ankles and calves, generally to the knee. Sometimes a second bandage is used above the knee if the thighs are also affected. Ace bandages, however, don't work terribly well around the bony areas of the legs, such as the backs of the knees, because they can't reach into the dips and hollows of the leg. Ace bandages **do** have valuable uses in conjunction with other treatments, though, as we shall see. But they don't work well alone as anything more than a very temporary aid.

PHYSICAL THERAPY

With all the recent talk about exercise and physical fitness, there's been a lot of interest focused on the therapeutic benefits of physical activity on varicose veins. As we've seen, the pumping action of the muscles is an important factor in the circulatory system. The more your muscles engage in vigorous activities, the better your entire circulatory system functions, and the faster and more efficiently your blood moves. Exercise improves muscle tone, so it takes less activity to start the muscle pumps working. The heart becomes stronger, better able to propel the blood.

That's not only a general prescription for better overall cardio-pulmonary health. It follows that specific exercises focusing on those areas most prone to varicose veins can actually slow down the process that causes them.

In Chapter 11 of this book, you'll find just this kind of well-balanced exercise program. It emphasizes repetitive, consistently practiced workouts that focus on the lower legs, the thighs, and the gluteals.

2. AGGRESSIVE TREATMENTS: TAKING THE VEIN OUT OF SERVICE

Varicose veins are a disruption to the normal functioning of the circulatory system. Instead of the blood flowing smoothly from the superficial veins to the deep veins, and then onward to the heart, it can become bogged down, pooling in the lower legs, moving back and forth within the veins. The net effect is one of inefficiency, leading to venous insufficiency.

The goal of aggressive treatment is to restore the system to its proper functioning by removing the defective veins from service, rechanneling the flow to healthier veins, and, in the bargain, restoring the appearance of the leg.

Once the vein is gone, it's no longer visible. In some cases treatment consists of eliminating the vein as a conduit for blood with injections; it no longer carries blood because it's no longer a hollow tube. In other cases the vein is actually removed from the tissues by surgical procedures.

Within these two broad categories of treatment, several options exist, most of them cosmetically effective.

ELIMINATING THE CONDUIT

Here, the solution to blood backing up and pooling in an incompetent vein is simple: Like a road that is too old and worn to carry traffic, you close it down, permanently.

For the tiniest veins, like spider veins, there are several options. But for the larger, true varicose veins, there are fewer choices.

SCLEROTHERAPY

One of the most useful procedures available (and one most misunderstood by the general public) is known as sclerotherapy, "sclero" meaning hardening or thickening, "therapy" meaning treatment. Sclerotherapy works by causing the affected vein, either spider vein or varicose vein, to harden and shrivel, closing the tube through which blood flows.

A mild chemical solution called a sclerosing agent is injected into the vein. The inner membrane of the vein becomes irritated by the solution, and the cells collapse, as do the walls of the vein, shrinking to almost nothing. The vein vanishes from view as it shrivels to a tiny thread of scar tissue under the skin.

Sclerotherapy, perhaps more commonly known by its other name, injection therapy, has been around for many years, in one form or another. The procedure has had a checkered past, and, while sclerotherapy as it exists today is vastly improved over its earlier incarnations, its past reputation lingers on in many people's minds. Problems plagued the treatment back then: poor results, frequent recurrence of varicose veins after treatment, bad reactions to the sclerosing agents, and often poor choices of likely candidates. Ironically, of all the treatment procedures available to doctors today, modern sclerotherapy holds the greatest promise for most sufferers of varicose veins, regardless of the scope of their condition.

Sclerotherapy's greatest advantage over both the electronic treatments (like electrodesiccation and laser therapy) and surgical alternatives is that it is the most adaptable of any procedure. From the smallest spiders on the face or thighs to the largest tortuous, dilated veins of the lower legs, sclerotherapy offers the best possible treatment used alone or in conjunction with other treatments. Larger veins are easy enough to inject; it's the smaller spiders that used to be beyond sclerotherapy's abilities. But with the advent of microsurgical techniques in the 1970s, that changed.

The doctors who specialized in "impossible" reconstructive surgery, like re-attaching a severed hand or foot, needed to develop miniature tools to reconnect myriad small nerves and tendons. These tools found their way into varicose vein procedures, as well as into other fields. Sclerotherapy was made practical for tinier and tinier spider veins.

Other improvements, both in the sclerosing agents themselves and in the procedures for injecting the solutions, have helped give sclerotherapy the ability to treat varicosities predictably and with long-term effectiveness. There's also been improvement in the ability to identify good candidates for the procedure, which has also led to better results.

In fact, in Europe, where sclerotherapy has been in widespread use for years, it's the therapy of choice, replacing surgery in the overwhelming majority of cases. In Great Britain, for example, sclerotherapy is used in more than 90% of all varicose vein procedures. And physicians are rediscovering sclerotherapy in the United States, as well.

SURGERY

Surgery is the most aggressive form of varicose vein treatment. It is reserved for the most specific cases, when the condition is so severe that no other form of treatment is likely to succeed. When properly used, surgery gives excellent results, and is the procedure of choice in many parts of the world for the treatment of varicosities. In other parts of the world, it is the treatment of second choice, usually after the possibility of sclerotherapy has been eliminated.

Surgery is usually used to remove the main superficial vein of the leg, the long saphenous vein, which runs the length of the leg from the groin to the ankle, when it proves faulty. Other treatment techniques, namely sclerotherapy, often fail with the long saphenous vein, due to the size of the vein, the pressures within it, and the body's relentless attempts to reopen the vein. (There are some limited instances when sclerotherapy is used for the long saphenous vein, but usually the doctor expects an 80% recurrence rate within five years after treatment.)

As with any other operation, varicose vein surgery depends the most on the judgment of the physician and his technical skill. First, the doctor must be certain that the patient is a good candidate for surgery, that the case before him will respond well to the procedure, and that the patient needs it. Even the most perfect operation can be a mistake on a patient who doesn't need it. And second, the surgeon must be familiar with every aspect of the operation, and skilled in its execution.

There are four basic surgical procedures for varicose veins, performed either alone or in combination. Some are older techniques, rarely practiced today.

EXCISION

Removing individual varicose veins. This procedure does not attempt to remove the long saphenous vein, but removes rather the smaller, visible branches. It typically will involve many cuts, but it doesn't cure the basic underlying causes of faulty valves, perforators, or the long saphenous vein itself.

LIGATION

Cutting and tying off the saphenous vein at the femoral junction in the groin, but not removing the vein from the leg. Used often in the past, now quite rare. Only somewhat effective, in specific cases. Some surgeons may combine it with multiple incisions.

LIGATION AND SCLEROTHERAPY

Tying off the long saphenous vein, as in ligation procedure, but with the addition of sclerotherapy to close the saphenous vein and its branches. Fairly good results. This procedure is very common in France. While it's generally an effective procedure, there is some incidence of recurrence.

LIGATION AND STRIPPING

In contrast to the previously discussed procedures, ligation and stripping, as it's most commonly called, is the most physiologically sound, and usually involves just two small incisions: one at the ankle, where the great saphenous vein joins the femoral vein, the deep-system vessel that runs into the vena cava and on to the heart. The surgeon first separates the long saphenous vein from its five branches and from the femoral vein in the groin, inserts a fine wire called a stripper into the saphenous vein itself, and then pulls. The stripper neatly pulls out the saphenous vein, tearing the small tributary veins up and down the vein's length. In practice, many surgeons complement this procedure with as many as fifteen to twenty incisions in each leg to remove branches and perforators. This operation can be fairly tedious, usually requiring a lengthy hospital stay, and is rather uncomfortable for the patient during that time and afterward due to the number of incisions that are made. Curiously, this longer procedure is wide-spread among various practitioners for reasons that have more to do with habit than effectiveness. The functional aspects are very well served, in that the circulatory problem is often eliminated, but the patient is in the awkward position of trading the unsightliness of vari-cose veins for the unsightliness of the scarring that multi-incisions may bring.

LIGATION AND STRIPPING WITH SCLEROTHERAPY

The procedure has several important advantages over the multi-incision procedures: scarring is minimal, time spent recovering is short (the technique requires you to be up and walking the same day for proper recovery) and chances for recurrence are much less. Research shows that, even with a minimum amount of finesse, the procedure is extremely effective. And, as we'll discuss in greater detail further on, ligation and stripping, combines with sclerotherapy, offers superior cosmetic results, due to the minimal amount of actual cutting the technique involves. **The best surgical procedure available today.**

THE LASER

Developed originally as a tool in physics research, the argon laser has found its way into the doctor's office for a variety of uses. Skin ailments, eye surgery, even experimental coronary surgery, are particularly suited to this sophisticated high-energy device that seems a little like something out of *Buck Rogers*. When it comes to small varicosities, the laser is quite effective, moreso than electrodesiccation.

Unlike electrodesiccation, where the energy isn't as well directed, the laser is focusable, narrowing its full power to hit a very small area, even if the vein is part of a very small network of spiders.

The laser works like this: A current is passed through a chamber containing argon or other gases, which produces light of uniform wavelength. (Ordinary light consists of many different wavelengths.) When this light, of a specific wavelength and carrying great amounts of energy, is trained on a red vein, the energy passes through the mostly colorless skin and is absorbed by the red blood cells in the vein. These cells heat up very quickly and cauterize the walls of the vein. The small spider shrivels to nothing and disappears from sight. The procedure is not painful; each "shot" from the laser feels like a pinprick. Tiny scabs will form over the spider vein, and after seven to ten days these will fall off. The vein will then vanish over a period of a few weeks.

The procedure is still new, and not well known outside medical circles. But studies into the effects of laser therapy for a variety of vascular blemishes on the face show that, out of a test group of one hundred subjects. 94% showed good to excellent results.

But laser therapy isn't the perfect treatment for all cases of spider veins and small varicosities. As in the various forms of electrodesiccation, there are limits on how large a vein can be and still be effectively treated. Doctors who use the laser report that, in order to achieve good results, the vein can't be much more than one-fortieth of an inch in diameter. Sometimes the laser destroys the pigmentation of the skin, leaving a small white spot where it was used. But all in all, the technique offers several important advantages over older techniques of electrocautery and fulgaration. Not only is the beam of light easier to use than an electric wire—it's more accurate and focusable—but the amount of energy delivered to the site of the vein can be much greater. The red light of the laser will pass through ordinary tissue harmlessly, attacking only the vein. Electrocautery can't distinguish between normal and abnormal tissues.

OTHER TECHNIQUES

ELECTRODESICCATION

This technique, discussed in the previous chapter on spider veins, is somewhat effective. An electric charge is delivered to the skin by means of a fine needle. The cells shrink and close, and the vein ceases to exist. It shrivels to a tiny fraction of its former diameter, and vanishes.

There are several kinds of electrodesiccation, but the principle remains the same. **Fulgaration** is a technique useful over a wider area. It employs an electrode much like a tiny spark plug; the instrument is held above the skin, and the current is "sprayed" over the area of veins the physician wants to remove.

Electrocautery involves a tiny, hairlike needle, inserted through the skin into the vein. Again, an electric current is applied. The vein shrivels and vanishes.

Both techniques are effective when used properly over a small area. Problems arise when the physician tries to eliminate a network of veins over larger areas. Here, pitting of the skin and scarring may result, along with small white speckles—discolorations of the skin that occur when too many healthy cells are destroyed along with the vein. Likewise, results may not be good if the vein you're trying to eliminate is smaller than the instrument. Again, the electric current, which can't distinguish healthy tissue from the tissue you don't want, can cause scarring that's almost as objectionable as the vein was.

EXOTIC TREATMENTS

In an age where technology is zooming, it's inevitable that medical procedures change and improve constantly, too. The techniques just described are always being refined in small increments, to be sure; but other techniques are emerging that defy any classification other than "exotic" or "experimental." Most of the following techniques will never make it to your doctor's office, but it's hard to predict which ones might be seen, or when they might be seen outside of the laboratory.

SUBCUTANEOUS PUMPS

Some researchers are experimenting with implanting tiny pumps below the surface of the skin to aid in propelling the blood through problem areas of the vein. Highly impractical at the moment, the technology is derived from recent developments in treating diabetes by pumping minute amounts of insulin into the system on a regular basis.

ELECTROTHROMBOSIS

New variations on a very old procedure. Electrothrombosis is an obsolete technology that is the grandfather of electrocautery (some of the old machines still stand in the corner of some hospitals). Using a wire to carry the electric current to the site of the varicose vein, the vein is burned away in a very tricky—and often ineffective—procedure. New variations are focusing on the use of microscopic filaments to carry the current. The wire is threaded through or near the affected vein and *zap!* the vein—in theory, at least—vanishes.

VALVE TRANSPLANTS

In this experimental technique, healthy valves from veins located elsewhere in the body are substituted for faulty ones in the deep-system veins. This treatment is probably overkill for the vast majority of varicosities, except in the most serious, life- or limb-threatening cases, and is attracting some interest in cases of post-phlebitic syndrome, where the valves in the deep-system veins have been destroyed by phlebitis, and no other cure is possible.

VALVE RECONSTRUCTION

Another highly experimental procedure that is generally reserved for serious cases of deep-system insufficiency. Here the microsurgeon actually tightens the faulty valve(s) at the site of the vein's insufficiency. Considering the size of a valve, this is no small accomplishment, but for exactly that reason this technique will probably never find its way into most treatment programs—at least, not until microsurgery becomes routine (if ever).

*   *   *   *   *   *

Now you know that varicose veins can be treated, and you know the general sorts of treatments available. In the following chapters, techniques will be discussed in greater depth so that you can help your doctor choose the treatment that's right for your particular case of varicose veins.

CHAPTER 7

SURGERY

WHEN SURGERY IS NECESSARY

Approximately ninety percent of all varicose veins can be treated without surgery. But what about the other ten percent?

In spite of all the advances in the procedures that doctors use to treat varicose veins, sometimes the best treatment—and the only real choice of treatment—is complete removal of the affected vein by surgery.

When the condition of the veins warrants it, surgery has important advantages over other methods of treatment. It has the most long-term, permanent effect that a doctor can perform. When a varicose vein is removed surgically, it's gone forever—if the procedure has been done properly.

In about one out of ten cases varicose veins **must** be treated by surgery. In these cases there is no other option likely to give results as good for as long, or as likely to restore the circulation of the leg to its prevaricosed condition.

In the great majority of these cases, the vein to be
removed is the long saphenous vein, the longest vein in
the human body. This vein runs from ankle to groin
along the inside of the leg, meeting the large deep
system vein of the leg, the femoral vein, at the crease
of the groin, at what's called the saphenofemoral junction. This rather complex crossroads joins the saphenous vein and several of its tributaries, all feeding
blood into the femoral vein for its further journey into
the inferior vena cava and the heart. If you've ever
worn bluejeans, you'll be able to locate the saphenofemoral
junction right below the inside corner of the front pocket.
There's a long saphenous vein in both legs, but it's rare
for both long veins to fail at the same time. (About 80%
of varicose vein surgeries are performed on one leg
only. The other leg will often follow, perhaps years
later, though sometimes it will not. It depends on the
patient's particular condition, age, history, and so on.)

Sometimes, surgery is performed on a main tributary of the long saphenous vein, the so-called short
saphenous vein, located in the calf area.

WHY MUST THE VEIN BE REMOVED?

Varicose veins are caused by the failure of the
valves in the veins of the legs. Because of the structure
of the veins, the failure of one valve will double the
stress on the valve below it, setting off a chain reaction
throughout the system, and eventually varicose veins
will develop. To correct the problem, that first faulty
valve at the level of the saphenofemoral junction—just
above the femoral vein—must be removed from service.
Sometimes it's the veins called perforators that fail first,
permitting reverse flow of blood from the deep to the

superficial system. This surge of blood balloons the saphenous vein outward, causing the valves to fail. This can happen alone, or with the failure of the saphenofemoral valve. The end result is the same.

When valves in the long saphenous vein have failed, the entire venous system of the leg is affected. The sheer weight of the column of blood from this large vessel will quickly overcome the valves of the smaller veins below, causing small varicose veins to appear all over the leg.

Though they may be obvious in many cases, there may be minimal visual clues that implicate the faulty valves in the long saphenous vein as the cause of the smaller varicose veins. It may take years for the long vein itself to become obviously varicosed. In the meantime you might be tempted to have the smaller, visible varicosities treated—but the results will be decidedly mixed if the main vein is affected. Because the basic cause still remains, more varicose veins will appear.

In the past (and even today, in special cases) other methods were used to treat the failure of the long saphenous vein without its surgical removal. Sclerotherapy was the most popular method used—again, with mixed results. While the theory is good, in practice the body's natural reaction to the closing of a large blood vessel like the long saphenous vein is eventually to reopen it. This is called recanalization, and it's a major cause of varicose vein recurrence. In European studies of thousands of sclerotherapy patients, 80% of patients who were treated with sclerotherapy for the failure of long saphenous veins experienced recanalization within five years. Their problems were back. (There are some cases where a doctor will elect schlerotherapy of the long saphenous vein, even today. If the patient is too sick for surgery, frightened of the procedure, or elderly then the five-year recurrence rate may not be of concern.

Sclerotherapy can be repeated as often as needed. Likewise, surgical procedures which save the long saphenous vein, like local excisions or ligations, will not treat the original cause, and may lead to eventual recurrence. But your doctor should always explain the risks and likelihood of recurrence.)

Surgical removal of the varicose long saphenous vein is the best solution when it is affected. It eliminates the problem valves by eliminating the problem vein. When the vein is gone, it can no longer back up into the smaller vessels, it can no longer cause blood to flow in circuitous paths in the wrong direction, and its varicosities cannot recur. It may seem ironic, but removing the main superficial path of the blood—now hopelessly inadequate—is the best way to force the body to find new, more efficient routes for the blood to flow into the deep venous system and help the circulatory system to function better.

THE HISTORY OF VARICOSE VEIN SURGERY

Centuries ago, doctors didn't understand the human body. They thought that the liver was the heart, the spleen was the brain, and that bleeding was a cure. They likewise had little knowledge of the workings of the venous system.

But varicose veins were a common affliction even in the earliest times, especially among the privileged, who spent a good deal of their lives being carried from place to place, and eating rich foods. (It has taken centuries for the rest of us to reach their level of development.) Because these privileged patrons could afford medical care when most common people couldn't, doctors were frequently called upon to treat varicose veins, and they used procedures that by modern-day standards were somewhat bizarre.

Hundreds of years later, with some understanding of the workings of the circulatory system and with the advent of anesthesia and crude antiseptics, surgery became an increasingly feasible treatment for many conditions. And when it came to varicose veins, surgery seemed like a good idea, too. So doctors tried it. They learned about varicose veins and surgery itself as they went along. Throughout the history of medicine, and the history of surgery as well, experience was used as the basis for experimentation. As surgeons learned, they added to their techniques. When they made a mistake, they learned from that, too.

At first, doctors tried to remove varicose veins wherever they saw them, in a technique called excision. It seemed to work, so the early surgeons expanded on the technique, removing more and more veins, until they devised a difficult and lengthy operation that consisted of one long incision from thigh to foot, along the route of the long saphenous vein. The veins were removed, and the leg was sewn back together.

The procedure was based not on any known principles of the circulatory system, but rather on the simple premise that if the surgeon removes the visible problem, the patient is cured. Due to the primitive conditions, however, many patients died, and more than a few lost their legs to infection. But in 1885, it was the best doctors could do.

Unfortunately, it wasn't long before these patients who had extensive stripping operations were back, with more varicose veins.

Clearly, simply removing the visible veins wasn't

working. There had to be an invisible cause of the problem somewhere else. Dr. Mayo of the famous Mayo Clinic discovered that the veins were recurring because the long saphenous vein and its valve at the groin (the root cause of the problem) were not removed. It became clear that any successful operation must remove the long saphenous vein from the saphenofemoral junction downwards.

Then, in the early years of the twentieth century, a Dr. Keller figured out how to remove the long saphenous vein without extensive incisions, in fact with only two small cuts. He made a small incision of the groin and at the ankle, located the vein, inserted a stiff wire into it, and pulled it—or stripped it—out. The procedure was called ligation (that is, cutting) and stripping, and it's the procedure practiced today, although now much refined.

Surgeons everywhere tried the procedure and found good results, and they altered and modified it, publishing papers to share the techniques, experiences, and clinical notes with their colleagues. Stripping was safe, and it worked better than anything else had.

If particular care was taken to tie off all five branches of the long saphenous vein as it met the femoral vein, recurrence wasn't a problem. A sloppy cut, or ligation, could miss one or more of these smaller veins, and those veins would take over the saphenous vein's function, get overloaded, and fail, just as the long saphenous vein had. When surgery fails today, it's usually due to the same problem.

As time passed, surgeons began to cut carefully and to tie off not only the five main branches at the groin, but also as many of the smaller tributaries and perforators as they could, in an attempt to curtail the chances of parallel veins to become varicosed. Then, they removed all the visible branches they could find, too. (After all, that had worked well for years.) The operations became almost baroque in their complexity. Fifteen or twenty different incisions, often more, were routinely being made and the net result of the procedure was—and still is today—extensive scarring up and down the leg.

While the physiological results of the procedure were usually satisfactory, the multiple incisions meant multiple scars, and to patients who had hoped to restore their appearance, disappointment in the cosmetic results was common.

The fact is that most of all varicose vein operations performed in the United States still use the technique of ligation and stripping with multiple excisions. It continues to be the best known, most widely practiced, physiologically sound technique, but, as far as cosmetic appearance goes, it is not one of the most satisfactory varicose vein procedures available.

In Europe, though, other approaches were being taken. Sclerotherapy had become popular after the Second World War, this time with better results than ever before. For the first time, doctors began to combine surgery with sclerotherapy. Surgery, usually ligation of the saphenous vein at the saphofemoral junction, would take the long vein out of commission, though often the vein wasn't removed from the leg—just tied off and left inoperative. Then sclerotherapy would be used to close it down together with the smaller visible tributaries. The procedure used the strengths of both techniques together, with fairly good results. Ligation and sclerotherapy, as it's known, is still used extensively in France.

So the happy marriage of a surgical procedure with sclerotherapy has brought us to the best combination possible. The most complete operation—**ligation and stripping**—combined with **sclerotherapy,** for the most comprehensive and cosmetically pleasing results.

The ligation and stripping procedure itself has been tremendously streamlined and simplified in the hands of the skilled surgeon. Only two incisions are made—one, ½ inch long at the ankle where the long saphenous vein ends, and the other 1 inch long at the saphenofemoral junction in the groin. After the insertion of the "stripper" tool, and the removal of the vein, the incisions are closed with just a few stitches. The whole process need take no more than a half hour.

With the use of reliable, modern **sclerotherapy** techniques, the doctor needn't treat the other existing tributaries by surgery. So there are fewer incisions in each operation.

The sclerotherapy part of these combined techniques will take place before as well as after surgery for the smallest spiders, the branches and perforators.

Two months after the surgery, once all bruising has disappeared, and the sclerotherapy has been completed, we expect a total disappearance of veins and spider veins, with virtually no trace of surgical scars.

The operation for the removal of the long saphenous vein was, in all respects, a major operation. General anesthesia was required, as was a hospital stay of up to a week. The patient spent days in bed, was required to wear elastic bandages for about two weeks afterward, and was out of commission for up to a month. Depending on the time of year the procedure took place, those two weeks after the operation could be uncomfortable, sticky, and itchy.

These various advances in varicose vein surgery have culminated in a new approach: **Ambulatory Surgery.** Ambulatory Surgery gives important advantages: Greater patient comfort, and a much faster recovery. Ambulatory Surgery is designed to get the patient up and walking just a few hours after surgery, going home the same day of the operation. Varicose vein surgery is very well-suited to these quick recovery techniques.

Ambulatory Surgery has become possible because of important advances in anesthesia, the art of putting the surgical patient to sleep during the operation. Today's anesthesiologist has several choices of substances that act quickly, but with a light touch, enabling the patient to be awake moments after the incisions are closed. Within just a couple of hours, all traces of drowsiness are gone, and the patient can move freely under his or her own power. Computerized monitors in the operating room allow the anesthesiologist to get immediate, accurate information about the patient's oxygen levels, respiration rate, heartbeat, gases in the blood, and blood pressure, making the anesthesia—usually the most delicate part of any operation—easier to regulate.

These combinations of techniques, on an ambulatory basis, mean shorter hospital stays, and shorter recovery, too. As little as two hours after leaving the operating room, the patient is free to go home, and is free to resume his or her normal daily activities as soon as the next day. Shorter hospital stays mean fewer complications; studies of more than 2,000 ambulatory surgery patients show that virtually none experience any of the common postsurgical infections, complications or other "normal" problems associated with major surgery. The fact is that the sooner you're up and around, the faster your recovery, and the healthier you'll be.[8]

Is Ambulatory Surgery for you?

If your doctor decides that surgery would be the most effective form of treatment, you must be in generally good health to undergo the procedure. That mean no heart disease, diabetes, kidney problems, or other serious conditions that might imperil your life when your body undergoes the added stress of an operation. You shouldn't be a smoker or a heavy drinker. Patients who regularly take medications should tell their physicians, as these medicines will have to be discontinued the night before surgery. Even modern forms of ambulatory surgery are a serious matter, not to be taken lightly. Anyone who goes "under the knife" should be prepared for the possibility of blood loss, an adverse reaction to anesthesia, difficulty in healing, or even (very rarely) the possibility of infection. If you are not in basically sound health, your doctor may decide that although surgery would otherwise be best, he can't risk it; a nonsurgical form of treatment may be recommended instead.

THE SURGICAL EXPERIENCE: GOING THROUGH IT

What is surgery like? What really happens when a patient is operated on for varicose veins? If you're a candidate for a modern ligation and stripping procedure, you'll be a hospital patient for only five or six hours, and within that time you'll be admitted, meet with your doctor, be anesthetized, operated on, and woken up, and will have recovered from anesthesia. By the middle of the afternoon (most surgery happens early in the morning), you'll be on the way home.

BEFORE THE PROCEDURE

Weeks before the surgery, your doctor and you will have reached the conclusion that the ligation and stripping procedure offers the best chance for correction of your varicose vein problem. Undoubtedly, your physical exam would have told your doctor that the long saphenous vein itself was involved, and no other form of therapy would work. A hospital date will be set shortly thereafter, and as the date approaches, arrangements will be made to have blood and urine samples taken. Any procedure involving anesthesia requires these tests, to help the anesthesiologist choose the appropriate forms of anesthetic for you, based on your medical history. Sometimes these blood and urine samples are taken at the hospital, but your doctor may take the samples in his office instead, usually a month to a week before your surgery is scheduled. Depending on your age, a chest X-ray and cardiogram may be done.

It's a good idea to keep in touch with your doctor in the days immediately before the procedure. If you have a cold, or if you're not feeling well, your doctor may want to reschedule for some other time. You should be in top shape the day of surgery; it makes everything else go more easily.

Many women patients worry about undergoing surgery if they are having their period. If everything else is otherwise perfectly normal, menstruation is nothing to worry about. In fact, surgery will very likely cause the onset of your period. It's the body's normal reaction to the stress of the procedure.

An important thing to remember about the day of surgery is that after you are released from the recovery room, a friend or companion should meet you in the hospital to make sure you get home all right. You may be very tired and achy, a little dizzy or disoriented. Arranging an escort is very important for your safety—so important that many ambulatory surgery units will cancel your procedure unless you've made plans for a responsible adult to accompany you home. Usually there's a comfortable place for your friend to wait until you're well enough to leave.

And remember: Don't eat anything or drink anything after midnight the night before your scheduled procedure. Food in the stomach can be very hazardous during anesthesia.

THE DAY OF YOUR SURGERY

Surgery is usually scheduled for early in the morning, so you'll be admitted to the hospital even earlier than that. If you've ever been to the hospital, you know that there are a lot of papers and forms to fill out. Make sure you bring your insurance ID card, as well as any insurance forms that might be applicable. If there's difficulty with the paperwork at the hospital, the result can be nerve-wracking and annoying. It's always best to check with the hospital to make sure you have everything you'll need for admission.

The day of the procedure, wear loose fitting, comfortable clothes. Loose clothing will be easier to put back on after surgery when you're likely to be sore and fatigued. Don't wear jewelry, makeup, nail polish, stiff shoes, or hosiery. High heels are unnecessary and likely to be painful as well. Also, don't carry large amounts of cash or valuables; a hospital is a large, busy place that cannot take the time or responsibility to keep track of them.

After admission, you'll be directed to the ambulatory surgery unit, given a hospital gown and asked to wait for your doctor to arrive. He or she will probably have been "suiting up" for the procedure, consulting with the anesthesiologist, and planning the procedure with technical support people who will all be present in the operating room with you.

You'll meet both your doctor and the anesthesiologist then. The anesthesiologist is a specialist in the art of putting people to sleep for surgery, and after asking you about your personal medical history (and comparing notes with your surgeon), will decide the most medically appropriate method that can be used to achieve a deep sleep that can be reversed quickly, with as few side effects as possible. There are many choices, so your own special "blend" will be custom-tailored, based on your personal state of health, the length of the procedure, and your personal preference. The anesthesiologist will usually brief you on what to expect from side effects from the medication. He or she will probably tell you to avoid driving for a day after the procedure, and what foods and drinks to steer clear of, too.

At this point, your doctor will again brief you on what will take place—the procedure, the expected recovery time, the way you'll feel when you wake up, what you should do in the first few days after you return home, how soon you can go back to work (generally from within a couple of days to a week) medications you'll be prescribed, and how soon you should come to the office for a postsurgical exam.

Soon you'll be taken to the operating room. In traditional surgery, the patient might be anesthetized before entering the operating room on a cart or "gurney." With ambulatory surgery, the patient usually just walks in. The operating room is a large room filled with electronic equipment, a large overhead light that the doctor will focus on the area he's working on, and a complicated-looking table in the center. There are likely to be quite a few people in the operating room preparing for their parts in the procedure: the anesthesiologist and his or her assistant, several nurses, orderlies and technicians, and your doctor, who is like the director of the show.

Under the intense glare of the operating room light,

your doctor will again examine your legs as you stand, this time marking the varicose veins with a pen or some other insoluble marker. Once you are prone on the operating table, your varicosities drain, and are difficult to see. He or she will pay particular attention to the junction of the saphenous and femoral veins at the groin, and to locate the junction, you'll be asked to cough as he or she feels for the valve reflux, the telltale backward flow of blood through a faulty valve at the junction. Once it's marked, the procedure is ready to begin.

ANESTHESIA

Now it's the anesthesiologist's turn to give you a last look. You'll be directed to lie down on the operating table, which will be tilted as instructed by your doctor. At the head of the operating table is the anesthesiologist's equipment for monitoring your progress and the effect of the drugs he or she is administering. Technicians will tape sensors to your skin connecting you to these machines.

Depending on the course of action the anesthesiologist has chosen, you may be given an injection, or an intravenous tube in the hand, dripping a relaxant or sleep-inducing agent slowly into your bloodstream, or some combination of methods to put you to sleep.

After you're asleep, the anesthetic may be switched to something even milder, to keep you just barely unconscious. The advantage of this approach is a quicker recovery at the end of the procedure, but once you're asleep, you'll not be aware of this change (or, for that matter, of anything else that will occur, until it's all over). A face mask or a throat tube may be used to keep the anesthetic gases flowing into your lungs.

THE PROCEDURE ITSELF

In the few minutes it takes for the anesthetic to take effect, your doctor is "scrubbing up" near the operating room, as are the assisting technicians and nurses. Tools are being arranged in preparation for the procedure. Once the anesthesiologist nods that he or she (and you) are ready, the surgery begins.

First, the entire leg, from hip to toe, is slathered with a brick-red iodine disinfectant. A small patch of pubic hair is shaved exactly above the femoral vein's connection with the saphenous vein.

Then your whole body is draped with green surgical cloths, leaving exposed only the parts that will actually be involved in the surgery (in this case, the site of incision at the groin and the inside of the ankle). The reason for this is hygiene: even the best-scrubbed skin contains germs that could cause infection if allowed into the area of the incision.

The table is tilted so that your feet are higher than your head, and the blood in your legs drains back to the heart. Now everyone in the operating room is ready for the surgery to begin.

The doctor cuts through the top layers of skin, exposing the tissue underneath. An electric cautery tool, about the size of a pencil, is used to seal the blood vessels under the skin and stop bleeding. The incision is made deeper, and the doctor's assistant helps by pulling back the tissue with retractors. In very little time, the doctor has reached the site of the critical saphenofemoral junction. The entire incision is a little over one inch long, and about an inch and a half deep.

The junction itself is not a simple Y-shaped intersection, but rather a more complicated one of several veins. The saphenous vein here has five tributaries branching away close to the connection to the femoral vein, and it's critical that all these tributaries be located and tied off, or—as surgeons found out many decades ago—the operation may fail.

So the next phase of the procedure is one of particularly close, delicate work. The doctor ties each of the smaller branches of the saphenous vein tightly with catgut and severs them from the main vein. Then the long saphenous vein itself—the trunk that all the branches spring from—is severed from the femoral vein.

Once the long saphenous vein has been severed from the femoral vein, the surgeon moves to the ankle where the saphenous vein ends, branching away into three smaller vessels. Here the incision is much smaller and not nearly so deep; the long saphenous vein lies directly below the surface and can be found quickly and easily. In seconds, the vein is exposed, its three branches tied off and cut. Here the incision is as small as ½ inch long.

Now the doctor takes the stripping tool and inserts it into the exposed end of the vein at the ankle. The stripper is little more than a stiff piece of nylon wire, like a heavy fishing line. It slips easily through the vein, until it comes out at the other end of the saphenous vein in the incision at the groin. The doctor takes the protruding end at the groin and snaps a small plastic knob onto it, about the size of a button. Then he pulls firmly, while a technician applies firm pressure along the path of the vein. The procedure is nearly completed now.

It just takes a minute for the doctor to pull the stripper the length of the entire leg. The branches of the saphenous vein, now severed by the stripper, will bleed a little, but will seal themselves very quickly. When the tip of the stripper, with the plastic knob, emerges from the leg at the ankle, it carries with it the entire long saphenous vein, now just a small lump of white tissue.

A few stitches close the wound at the groin, even fewer the ankle. These are placed under the skin, so you can't even see them. Elastic bandages are wrapped from ankle to thigh. The anesthesiologist reverses the medications. Groggy, you awaken. The surgery is over. Total time elapsed since surgery began: under an hour. After a recovery time of only two or three hours, you can walk home, and return to work after a few days.

RECOVERING FROM THE OPERATION

After you awaken in the ambulatory surgery recovery room, there may be some soreness, the kind you might expect from a bruise, and some black-and-blue marks. They will probably be with you from several days to two to four weeks, but will gradually fade away.

You'll be given a prescription for a mild pain reliever, and taking one or two the day of your surgery is usually sufficient.

Your leg will be wrapped with an Ace bandage, and there will be small bandages on your groin, at the site of the incision. You may feel groggy or disoriented, but your head will clear quickly. It's important to get back on your feet quickly, and the nurses in the recovery room will encourage you to walk around as soon as you're able. If everything is otherwise normal, you'll be released to a friend or companion just a couple of hours after the surgery.

AS YOUR RECOVERY CONTINUES

Once you're home, you can resume your regular daily activities as soon as you feel up to it. Some people go to work the next day, though you may feel that that's pushing it. Maybe you'll want to take a couple of days off, but that doesn't mean lying in bed all day. We think that walking—and walking far—is an important factor in a quick, healthy recovery. Walk as far as you possibly can, several miles a day in the days following the operation. The more you walk, the faster your recovery will be. If you want to rest, always elevate your legs.

After you've had an ambulatory procedure, your doctor will likely ask that you leave on the small bandage at the groin and ankle for about forty-eight hours after the surgery. The Ace bandages should stay on until your doctor examines you after the procedure, usually within three to five days. If you experience pain after the operation, aside from the general soreness, it's possible that these bandages are too tight. (They should be snug, but what seems snug to your doctor in the operating room might be uncomfortable to you.) If they're too tight (or too loose, for that matter) you can simply remove them and rewrap them—snugly, but comfortably.

The first time you unwrap your legs, you may see black-and-blue bruising up and down the leg. This bruising is entirely normal and, considering that you've just had the major superficial vein of the leg removed, is a minor discomfort that will heal, just like any other bruise, over the next three or four weeks.

At your first postoperative visit to your doctor, you'll be examined, and any further course of treatment can be outlined then. Ambulatory surgery patients will have those remaining varicose branches removed by sclerotherapy in short order in a few office visits. This is also the time you can discuss with your doctor your progress and ask any questions you may have about your recovery.

The return to your normal life is progressive, starting

on your first day after surgery. Eat and drink whatever you like, and go wherever you want. But keep an eye to continuing some basic commonsense maintenance routines such as keeping off your feet if you can, resting with legs raised, and including a moderate exercise program in your daily activities.

COMPLICATIONS OF SURGERY

There are risks associated with any surgery that also apply to surgery for varicose veins.

The patient must be in reasonably good health because anesthesia is stressful, even for healthy people. Surgeons speak of anesthesia the way pilots speak of takeoffs and landings; the flight itself is usually uneventful, but it's getting up and coming back down that's the most delicate part.

Smokers should refrain from lighting up for a good two weeks prior to surgery because the effects of cigarette smoke on the lungs makes respiration during anesthesia more difficult. Likewise, alcoholics and heavy drinkers make the appropriate dosages of anesthetic into guesswork; their bodies are so used to stupor-causing drugs already that it takes more "punch" to put them under.

Some patients may be too frail or too old to undergo the operation, and their life expectancy might influence a doctor's decision to forego surgery as a treatment. Why put a 78-year-old to risk for a procedure that will give results that last for fifty years, when one that will be effective for five years will very likely be satisfactory?

And there are some people who are simply so frightened by the idea of "going under the knife" that the advantages of the operation are outweighed by the emotional stress of worrying about it.

There are also several possible complications that can occasionally occur during or after any surgery, varicose vein surgery included.

BLEEDING. Bleeding is extremely rare. Controlling the bleeding is usually an easy matter, done with sutures. Usually the only noticeable effect of bleeding is black-and-blue bruising.

INFECTION. Despite the precautions taken at hospitals today, in rare cases, infections can flare up at the incision sites. Antibiotics are prescribed at the first sign.

SCARRING. Improper healing of the incision sites can occasionally result in a noticeable scar. This problem is of more concern the more incisions there are, and may be a disconcerting or disfiguring reminder of the surgery after it's over. Most scars do fade by themselves in time, often over several months.

BRUISING. A nuisance more than a lasting side effect, black-and-blue bruises will usually heal over three to four weeks' time. The accompanying soreness will also ease.

RECURRENCE. With the underlying cause of varicose veins gone, recurrence is not likely, except in the case of smaller branches that may occasionally make themselves visible. Today, these are easily treated, as are the occasional spider veins that may also crop up.

The vast majority of surgeons—more than 99.9%—are competent professionals with a deep and thorough understanding of the structure of the leg and the proper procedures to treat that structure. But there have been instances of gross malpractice, and with the legal and medical fields being in the news frequently, you should know that mistakes have occurred. Surgeons have removed arteries instead of veins, and lost patients during the simplest procedures imaginable. Make sure your physician has a good reputation, and is a member of the local medical society. This advice goes for anyone going to any doctor, whether surgeon, dentist, or general practitioner, for any reason.

Surgery is the best treatment for certain cases of varicose veins, but there are different approaches to the procedure that have evolved over time. Each started from a desire to achieve the best results for the sufferer of varicose veins. It's only recently that the techniques have reached the point where both the physiological and the cosmetic benefits are balanced. Ligation and stripping, especially when done on an ambulatory basis in conjunction with refined sclerotherapy techniques, is the closest thing we have to a perfect combination of procedures for advanced varicose veins. But most Americans are unaware of it, and this approach is used in just a few medical centers on the East and West Coasts, and perhaps a few in between.

Soon ambulatory surgery for varicose veins will become more widespread. If patients ask their doctors, then it will become available more quickly. So speak to your doctor and discuss the options available. Be an informed consumer of medical treatment, not just a patient.

CHAPTER 8

SCLEROTHERAPY: EFFECTIVE THERAPY THAT EMPHASIZES COSMETIC RESULTS

Sclerotherapy has been around ever since the invention of the hypodermic needle, back in the 1850s. Some historians believe sclerotherapy was one of the first things physicians used the new device for. The idea seemed simple enough: inject a medication into the varicose vein that would shrivel up the vein from the inside, expel the stagnant pools of blood, curing the condition. Doctors started the search for appropriate solutions to inject into their patients' veins, and quickly ran into a serious obstacle. Most of the solutions they tried were too harsh, causing horrible blood clots or burns. More than a few of those hapless early patients died of poisoning or heart failure as their doctors experimented. Needless to say, sclerotherapy was not viewed as a viable form of treatment in the late nineteenth century, and as soon as procedures were developed for anesthesia and sterilization, physicians began to see surgical removal of varicose veins as a safer bet.

Some doctors, though, like the *idea* of sclerotherapy,

even if in practice the technique was flawed. Sclerotherapy was such a neat, clean concept—no messy surgery, no lengthy hospitalization, no scars or infections, potentially few side effects; if only it worked. Over the next thirty or forty years, the search continued for more effective (and less dangerous) sclerosing solutions, as well as for improved procedures for administering them.

In the late 1930s and on into the early '40s, newer solutions were found, and sclerotherapy again became popular with doctors seeking an alternative to complicated surgical procedures. Doctors had been operating on varicose veins for years and were growing tired of the limitations. These were the days of multi-incision operations that often left patients looking worse than they did before surgery. These were the days of crude anesthesia, lengthy hospital stays, and all too common complications. So when improved injection techniques became known, many doctors jumped on the bandwagon and injected almost anyone who walked in the door.

The medical community is often as influenced by fashion as anyone else. The drawback of this sort of whimsy is sometimes a lack of understanding of new, stylish treatments. As the pendulum swung the way of sclerotherapy over the next twenty years, and as doctors injected many patients who perhaps shouldn't have been injected, results suffered. Many cases of varicose veins, treated with injections of the newer solutions, vanished for a short period of time, and then reappeared. Patients were understandably upset and angry. Physicians, not understanding the reasons for the recurrences, became upset as well. The early promise of sclerotherapy was—again—broken. American doctors returned to the more predictable (though more aggressive and sometimes traumatic) option of surgery, and the general population either forgot about sclerotherapy, or thought of it as the procedure that didn't work very well and was used by quacks.

Meanwhile, social conditions and governmental policies of several European nations led physicians overseas to explore further the art of sclerotherapy, for several reasons. After the war, these European countries adopted various forms of socialized medicine, in which doctors are paid for their services by the government. What does socialized medicine have to do with varicose veins? Simple—when medical care becomes very cheap for the patient, the patient is more likely to seek out treatment for all kinds of "minor" problems, varicose veins being one—and that starts to get expensive for whoever is footing the bill, in these cases, the government. The governments involved, in England and Scandinavia especially, started to look for cheaper ways to treat varicose veins, so as to free up surgeons and hospital beds for the more seriously ill.

At the same time, another powerful social force in France contributed to the refining of sclerotherapy techniques: haute couture. Because the French were always so conscious of fashion, it seemed only natural that they paid very close attention to the look of a woman's legs under a pair of sheer hosiery. Much as the French were world leaders in cosmetics for the face, they became leaders in the cosmetic uses of medicine to beautify the appearance of legs. Indeed in France today are the only doctors who identify themselves as exclusively varicose vein specialists. They are known as *Phlebologistes* and they do nothing but.

Doctors tried different ways of administering sclerosant solutions, and their experience translated into the better, more effective techniques that inspired a revival of sclerotherapy procedures in Europe. The same techniques, and variations on those techniques, have begun to surface in the United States in the last decade. Only now are they filtering down to the general public.

The big difference between sclerotherapy techniques now and then is the sclerosing solutions, administered with better understanding, and refined techniques. Today's solutions are substances that act only on the walls of the veins; they don't clot the blood in the veins. (When the vein's walls contract, they force the blood out of them.) Today's solutions are also purer, and more controllable, due to improved laboratory techniques, and the art of determining the proper dosage is much refined, as a result.

The history of sclerotherapy is very much a history of the solutions themselves. In the earliest days of the procedure, doctors tried many different kinds of agents to shrink the veins. They used quinine, and salicylic acid (a relative of aspirin). And they also tried saline solutions, and glucose, too. They finally arrived at the group of substances known as fatty acids, derived from animals (cod liver oil was a favorite substance which could be processed down to its fatty acid components) which offered fairly good results compared to what had gone before. The problem with the first fatty acids was their variation in strength, and the stray impurities— tiny bits of errant proteins—that would sometimes cause unpredictable allergic reactions.

Then in the late 1930s and early 40s, scientists devised the first synthetic fatty acid, and used it in a solution called soltradecol, which is still used widely today. Soltradecol was an important advance for sclerotherapy, because it offered a pure, man-made solution with no impurities, and hence no unpredictable and undesirable side effects.

Combined with today's advanced techniques of diagnosis, injection, compression, more accurate dosages, and better understanding of which kinds of varicose veins are most likely to be successfully treated, sclerotherapy has reached what many had always predicted its true potential to be. After twenty-odd years of studies, sclerotherapy techniques can be compared favorably with surgical techniques in terms of medical effectiveness, and—when used properly on the right patients at the right time—are markedly superior in cosmetic terms to most surgical techniques.

How does an actual sclerotherapy session work?

First, whether or not you are a candidate for sclerotherapy depends on your condition; that is, your age, your general state of health, and the extent of your varicosities. Some people may be poor candidates for sclerotherapy, but there aren't many of those. One of the most remarkable aspects of sclerotherapy is the suitability of so many people to be treated by it. As long as your physician can find your varicose veins on your legs, he can, generally, inject them.

Often the physician will map out your venous system with markers, right on the leg. Some physicians will use iodine (a disinfectant) to trace the routes of your varicose veins as you are standing up. Whatever method is used, the purpose is the same. When you lie down, as most people do when the injections are administered, it's often difficult to find the veins, so they must be mapped out ahead of time. Photos are used to record the extent of the condition, and these will be referred to as treatment continues, as a record of what existed before treatment started, and how it should proceed. More photos may be taken during the course of treatment. Some doctors keep files of before and after photos to show prospective patients.

Now the physician selects a likely site to begin the injections, based on what's been determined about your basic anatomy. Using the fingers, pressure is applied an inch or two above and below the injection site. This will effectively close off the blood flow through the vein, as well as prevent blood from dribbling in from above the site through a faulty valve.

The vein is now ready. A fine needle, filled with a dilute solution of the sclerosing medication, is inserted into the vein, through the top layer of skin. The physician draws back on the plunger, watching the hub of the needle for the telltale drop of blood that indicates the needle has found the vein. Pushing in very slowly, the clear sclerosing solution enters the varicose vein. Because most sclerotherapists use extremely fine needles, the process is not painful, feeling instead like a tiny pinprick.

As seen from the physician's perspective, sclerotherapy is a small medical miracle. (Because the patient is usually lying down during the treatment, he or she usually can't see; the injections take place out of the patient's view.) As the plunger goes in, the sclerosing solution visibly expels trapped blood from the vein, or, in the case of a fine net of spider veins, from large parts of the spidered area. In seconds, a several square-inch area can be completely cleared of any sign of varicosity. As the treatment continues, and more injections are given, larger areas are cleared, as if someone took an eraser and rubbed the page clean.

Sometimes the doctor will start the series of injections at a site far away from the visible varicosities, in order to close off the area from the flow of blood. For instance, he might start in the area just below the groin to treat varicose veins that appear in the region of the knees.

The doctor standing at the patient's side during the procedure, quickly presses a disinfectant-soaked cotton ball onto the site of the injection as the needle is removed. This pressure keeps blood from reentering the injected vein and halts any bleeding.

After the injections, the leg is wrapped with an Ace bandage. If the injection site is localized, the bandage will be wrapped only around the immediate area. The patient is encouraged to walk around, in order to stimulate the circulation.

After the patient goes home (or back to the office—sclerotherapy is strictly an out-patient procedure that requires no recovery time) and the bandage is removed, (after about two hours) the sclerosed veins reappear somewhat as they fill up with blood again. It'll take three to four weeks for the veins to gradually fade away. From that point on, there is usually little sign that they were ever there.

Depending on the scope of the varicosities, the injections can be repeated in series, one after the other, until the entire leg is treated. The timetable of treatment varies: some doctors (and patients) may wish to get it all over with in a few visits of many injections each, while others may want to stretch the process out over more visits of fewer injections. Because the results are not affected by the time frame, it's usually entirely up to you and your doctor. In severe cases that may involve many veins and many spiders, the doctor may go along systematically, starting with the bigger veins first, then focusing on leaky valves, and finally proceeding to the smaller veins. But every case is different, and your doctor may tailor his or her technique to get the best result.

Not all veins will respond immediately. Veins that do not respond to the first treatment are treated again at the next visit using a slightly stronger solution. By repeating treatments, the doctor is able to find the exact dilution that is effective for each vein.

COMPRESSION: THERE ARE SEVERAL OPTIONS

Sometimes, your doctor's particular philosophy of sclerotherapy will dictate how he approaches your treatment. Just as there are differing opinions in the medical community about the ways to treat any disease, there are differing schools of thought about sclerotherapy itself.

Remember: sclerotherapy's history was spotty. So when the procedure was revived the latest time, doctors tried to **improve** the procedure by combining it with a technique known as **compression**. In other words, this time around, they weren't taking any chances on sclerotherapy's success.

A standardized procedure of Compression Sclerotherapy was designed to take some of the doubt out of sclerotherapy, and it was studied by a number of doctors in large scale tests in England, Canada, and Scandinavia. The Fegan technique, named after the British physician, Dr. W. G. Fegan described a procedure by which a 3% solution of soltradecol was injected into the vein, and then, immediately after, the leg was tightly wrapped with an Ace bandage, supplemented by support hose, and remained tightly wrapped for six to eight weeks. The theory behind this rather rigorous procedure is sound: the emptied vein stays empty, and the vein's inner walls stay in contact with each other. By pressing the walls of the vein together with the elastic bandage, they fuse, resulting in a "cleaner" thread of scar tissue. During the six-week wrapping period, patients were told to walk one or two miles each day (regardless of the weather) in order to encourage the legs' circulatory system to find new routes for the blood flow back to the deep system of veins.

The technique worked very well, and was eagerly adopted by physicians in many countries. One study showed that out of a large group of patients treated at a Canadian clinic, two years following treatment 84% of the patients said their legs felt better, while 81% reported that they looked better. Ninety percent of these patients said that, should they ever need more treatment, sclerotherapy was fine with them. Only 7% of these patients would have preferred surgery.[9]

Unfortunately, the wrapping portion of the Fegan technique was awkward for both patient and practitioner. So uncomfortable was the wearing of constricting bandages for so long a period of time that even in the pioneer studies of the procedure no treatment was attempted in either the summer months (because of the heat) or in the dead of winter (patients had to walk miles every day and that was difficult with snow and ice on the ground).[10]

So, as doctors do when they have a question to answer, they did more research. Another study compared the effects of wrapping the legs for different periods of time after the injection of sclerosant solutions. Conclusion: Reducing the bandaging time actually improved the results.[11] Today's sclerotherapy techniques use dramatically shorter compression times—as little as two or three hours.

Today's modern sclerotherapy technique also uses extremely mild and dilute sclerosing solutions, compared to the compounds used just ten years ago. Microdose sclerotherapy has many advantages over other injection techniques, and few side effects, and even milder, more controllable action. By repeating the treatments, a vein can be injected several times over a period of several weeks, instead of one strong shot followed by a six-week wait to see if it worked, as Fegan's technique required. Because the solutions are so mild, they can be used successfully to treat spider veins, as well as true varicosities. Stronger solutions would tend to burn and scar a very tiny blood vessel, along with the surrounding tissues, causing discoloration and cell damage. Because the injections are so mild, they can be administered repeatedly. The dosage can be easily strengthened in tiny increments, until any blood vessel's precise threshold is found. This gives the physician a great deal of flexibility in designing a treatment program for any individual patient. The result of this ''slow and steady'' technique is therefore very predictable and pleasing. Patients are usually very happy with the way their legs look and feel.

Yes, sclerotherapy is effective, when used properly. But it is not a cure-all, and it is **not** effective when the long saphenous vein itself is faulty, nor when the main valve in the groin is faulty, nor when multiple ''perforator'' veins (those vessels that connect the superficial veins to the deep system) are faulty. Those cases represent about 10% of varicose vein patients, and 80% of those people, when treated with sclerotherapy, will show good results for less than five years before recurrence of the problem. These 10% are the patients who should be treated surgically, perhaps with sclerotherapy as a combined therapy.

POSSIBLE SIDE EFFECTS OF SCLEROTHERAPY

Sclerotherapy, while being a major advance in the treatment of varicose veins (indeed, over 90% of varicose vein sufferers can be effectively treated by it), is not a cure-all with no negatives. Luckily, for most people, side effects are rare and, in the majority of cases where side effects do occur, they are very mild—a bruise or soreness at the injection site. The usual treatment for such soreness is time; just like a regular bruise, these will usually heal themselves. But there are some patients—a very tiny percentage of cases—that suffer from somewhat more serious effects.

INFLAMMATION. Sometimes, after the sclerosant solution is injected into two ends of a blood vessel, blood is trapped in the middle with no place to go. This is called localized phlebitis (the term means "inflammation of the vein" and has no relation to dangerous deep-vein phlebitis, except linguistically) and the symptoms include soreness, and discoloration of the surrounding tissues. Out of 533 patients treated by sclerotherapy in a recent study, 60 reported mild localized phlebitis, of which only 3 were considered significant. Even these went away by themselves, the study reported.[12]

The doctor has several options in cases of localized phlebitis, including drawing the trapped blood out, or doing nothing, and waiting for the body to reabsorb it. The blood turns black, and looks like oil. If the blood has accumulated for a long period of time, the presence of iron in the blood may discolor the surrounding tissues, though this staining usually vanishes on its own after several months, depending on the severity of the condition. Cosmetic coverups can help hide the marks until they disappear.

ALLERGIC REACTIONS. This side effect is quite rare today, thanks to the new synthetic fatty acids used in the injecting solutions. In sclerotherapy's earlier days, however, errant proteins—impurities in the sclerosants—caused occasionally massive and serious reactions.

In very few cases, however, a patient may develop an allergic reaction to the synthetic solution. Usually this occurs in one patient out of many thousands, and the reaction is generally mild. A slight rash or flush may appear, and the usual treatment of a common antihistamine will clear up the reaction in a few minutes.

SCABBING. Even less often, a tiny scab, similar in appearance to a cigarette burn, may form at the injection site. It's a reaction to the solution, and will heal by itself in three to four weeks. Again, scabbing was more common with sclerosing solutions of decades past, when not only were solutions stronger, but dosages were less precise. With the advent of milder, more artfully controlled dosages, this side effect has become a rarity.

DISCOLORATION. When we speak of discoloration in relation to sclerotherapy, we are really speaking of two distinctly different conditions, with different causes.

The first kind of discoloration, or pigmentation, is today quite rare, again because of the vast improvements doctors have made in the sclerosant solutions. Years ago, when doctors were matter-of-factly injecting strong dosages of animal-based fatty acids, the trauma of the chemicals under the skin often produced reactions and scabbing, and with (though occasionally without) these accompanying symptoms the skin would produce higher concentrations of melanin, the coloring agent of the skin. These melanin stains appeared as darker areas around the site of the injections. After a period of time, often about a year, the skin would reabsorb the melanin and the stain would vanish. But with the newer, gentler solutions, these chemically induced stains are seldom seen today.

However, in certain cases of varicose veins, irritation, or inflammation, or several other factors over a long period of time can produce the same kind of melanin stain in the skin in the area of the varicose vein. Again, it will usually fade after a period of time, though now so-called "bleaching agents" will reduce the production of melanin and fade the stain.

The second kind of pigmentation is caused by another process, involving the gradual often unnoticed seepage of blood under the surface of the skin, usually as the result of long-existing varicose veins. This blood is mostly reabsorbed; but the iron in the blood remains in the tissues near the surface, causing a brownish discoloration. Ironically, the existence of these stains is often unrecognized until after treatment is complete. Once the purplish discoloration of the varicose veins themselves are removed, the iron stains become visible. The stains are not caused by the treatment; the treatment just reveals them to the eye.

Alas, nothing really can be done about these stains. Dermabrasion, where a part of the skin is removed by either chemical or mechanical means, can occasionally help, but by no means is the treatment a sure thing.

OTHER HAZARDS. There are some other extremely rare hazards associated with sclerotherapy, but before you read about them, please understand that they are, for all practical purposes, unheard of except in scholarly journals. They are presented here to inform you that sclerotherapy, like every other medical procedure—even the most innocuous ones—can be dangerous if improperly practiced.

Occasionally a sclerosing needle may miss its intended target. When the vein to be treated is a small one, the few drops of solution may cause damage to the healthy cells surrounding the vessel, leaving a sore that may be slow to heal. If the vein to be treated is a larger one, a mistake like this can be very serious, resulting in extensive scarring. Treatment for ulcers of this type includes medicated bandages and constant care. Alert your doctor if you suspect you have an ulcer.

There are even cases of physicians mistakenly injecting sclerosing solution into active arteries, causing major damage. Severe anaphylactic shock, an allergic reaction to animal-based sclerosants, is a very rare, life-threatening side effect that has occurred perhaps three or four times in forty years to sclerotherapy patients. Sclerotherapy is overwhelmingly safe if properly administered, but such tragic freak occurrences do exist. Make sure your doctor, as any other doctor you may see for any problem, is properly accredited.

Sclerotherapy is not a cure for varicose veins, as we have said. Some patients seem to think of it as a "shot" that immunizes them from more veins forming, and they are confused and upset if varicose veins continue to form. Sclerotherapy is a way to control and remove existing varicose veins, but it does not solve the basic inherited tendency that causes some people to develop varicosities. Those root causes are of a more fundamental nature, and have more to do with the structure of your circulatory system, the veins, and the valves, as well as your daily habits, your diet, your weight, and your inherited genetic makeup, which, no matter what you do, can cause other varicose veins to appear.

But sclerotherapy is an excellent way to deal with the varicose veins you have now. By eliminating the visible varicosities, and by treating varicosities early before they become major problems, it's a valuable and important technique that has finally—after one hundred years of development and disappointment—proven itself to be safe, reliable and effective, when used the proper way by the proper people.

Surprisingly few people who suffer from varicose veins know that. But they should.

CHAPTER 9

A VISIT TO YOUR DOCTOR

What can you expect when you do decide to seek professional help? Of course, a lot depends on who you see. Until very recently in the United States, varicose veins have not been the exclusive province of any one medical specialty (though in France, varicose vein specialists have been around for years; they're called *phlebologists*). Vascular surgeons, dermatologists, general surgeons, even internists and general practitioners may all offer some form of treatment.

How should you choose a doctor? It's important to remember that doctors are people just like anybody else, and they may be biased in one direction or another, just like anybody else. A doctor's training, experience, skills, ambitions, and degree of success all influence the treatment methods he or she prefers. Just because one particular treatment may be the best for you doesn't necessarily mean every doctor will recommend it.

For instance, vascular surgeons may treat varicose veins only reluctantly. Their field of expertise covers all the structural circulatory problems from varicose veins, at one end, to the most serious arterial diseases on the other. If a patient suffers from a life-threatening aneurysm of the aorta (the major artery that carries blood away from the heart) the vascular surgeon may be called upon to implant an artificial aorta. To a doctor who practices this often dramatic life-and-death specialty, common varicose veins may seem mundane, and some vascular surgeons may not devote much attention to them. And because a vascular surgeon is primarily a surgeon by training, it would not be unusual for such a doctor to lean heavily toward surgical procedures to correct a varicose vein condition, even if other methods might be as effective. Some vascular surgeons may practice sclerotherapy as an adjunct to surgery, but the focus of their interests may not be equal to a doctor who practices sclerotherapy all the time.

Dermatologists are often called upon to treat spider veins. Most are well versed in electrodesiccation techniques for tiny spiders, and some are highly skilled in sclerotherapy for larger spiders and smaller varicosities. But should a dermatologist attempt to treat more serious varicose veins? It would depend on his training and experience. Because a dermatologist may have little experience with surgery, he might have a bias against it, and that bias might affect his judgment in those borderline cases where surgery might be appropriate. Would a dermatologist recommend a good vascular surgeon if the case was beyond his skills? Or would he follow a perhaps biased course of treatment?

The same might be asked of internists or general practitioners. If varicose veins are not very common in their practice, the skills—and judgment—needed might not be as finely honed as a physician who treats a wide spectrum of varicose veins all the time. It's like anything else—he who does it the most, probably does it the best. In medical matters, the principle holds true.

Contact your local medical society for the names of doctors, clinics, hospitals, and practices that specialize in the treatment of varicose veins. For more information about how to find these doctors, refer to the Resources section in this book. Then choose carefully; ask for references and call them up.

Ask them questions that will tell you about their approach to varicose vein treatment. For instance, find out what your doctor's background is; is he or she a surgeon by training? A general practitioner? An internist? Then investigate further: if he's a surgeon, how often does he rely on surgical procedures for his patients? Is he familiar with nonsurgical techniques? What's his opinion of these other techniques? What surgical procedures is he familiar with—how many incisions will he make in your operation? Is it an ambulatory procedure, or does it require a hospital stay? How often does he perform this procedure?

What are your doctor's attitudes toward nonsurgical procedures? Does he use sclerotherapy, and if so, what is the percentage of his patients he uses it for? Perhaps he uses it exclusively. Does he subscribe to long-term compression sclerotherapy, requiring six weeks of bandaging, or the newer procedures that use bandages for only a few hours? What sorts of solutions does he use? What is the recurrence rate for his patients treated by sclerotherapy? What is his success rate? What is the range of varicosities he will treat by sclerotherapy? In his opinion, is sclerotherapy ever inappropriate? What would he then recommend if it was inappropriate?

Is your doctor familiar with other methods of eliminating the smallest spider veins, such as electrodesiccation or the argon laser? What is the availability of this equipment, and is he or his staff trained in its use?

Does your doctor rely on one form of therapy only,

or does he or she use various procedures together, such as surgery complemented by sclerotherapy, or sclerotherapy combined with laser?

And finally, to what degree does your doctor consider cosmetic results when choosing any procedure? Does the physiology of the circulatory system in the affected area take precedence over the way it will look after treatment, or does the appearance of the area come first, even if the underlying function of the veins suffers? Or do both appearance and function carry equal weight?

Based on questions like these, you should be able to make an informed decision. The doctor you choose should offer a balanced treatment program, customized to each individual patient. He should not rely too heavily on any one procedure because he is deficient in another, but he should be highly skilled in all. All the techniques he uses should be thoroughly up-to-date. He should be treating many patients with similar conditions in his practice, as this will assure you that his skills are sharply honed. He should mix and match procedures easily, and be well informed of the limitations of each procedure, so that it is clear when one technique should be used over another. His techniques should favor neither function nor appearance at the sacrifice of the other. Both aspects of treatment should be given equal weight.

When you do choose your physician, your first office visit will be the most important. This is the doctor's introduction to you and your condition, and based on your doctor's findings at this first exam, it's where you and your doctor will plan your treatment. Here's what you can expect to be asked, regardless of what particular specialist you choose.

WHAT'S YOUR HISTORY?

The first thing any physician will ask you for when you arrive at his or her office is a general medical history. While you may think you have varicose veins, a good doctor will assume nothing. You'll be asked about illnesses you've had in the past, as well as any you may suffer from now. Have you ever been diagnosed for diabetes, high blood pressure, heart problems, hepatitis, asthma? Your answers to these questions will help your doctor put together a medical picture that will determine your diagnosis and treatment.

For instance, a middle-aged diabetic with varicose veins may experience several symptoms of poor circulation in the lower extremities that have nothing to do with varicose veins. And if surgery is indicated in this patient, a physician may think twice before operating, because of the fragile state of health and slow healing that often accompanies diabetes.

Likewise, heart problems may cause poor circulation in the lower limbs. Patients whose symptoms seem to point to varicose veins may really suffer from serious deep-system insufficiencies like phlebitis. Patients with infectious hepatitis may require treatment that would protect the medical staff from infection.

Do you suffer shortness of breath? Chest pains? Stomach problems? Blood in the urine? Have you ever had surgery? Do you take birth control pills? Do you take any other medications? Your doctor will also want to know if you've ever been treated before for varicose veins. If you have, he'll want to know about the history of that treatment. Did it not work well? What was the problem? Did the problem recur, and if so, why?

All these questions are designed to inform your

doctor, to let him know you better medically, to alert him to any possible underlying causes of your problem, and to direct him to a treatment program that's right for you.

WHAT ARE YOUR SYMPTOMS?

The next thing you'll likely be asked is to describe your complaint. Do your suspected varicosities hurt, or are they just unsightly? If you experience pain or heaviness, when does it occur? What makes the discomfort feel better? Did the pain come on gradually or all of a sudden?

After the interview, you will be escorted to an examination room, and after disrobing, usually from the waist down, your physician and/or your physician's assistant will make a visual assessment of your condition. He will begin a brief physical examination. The doctor will take pulse readings from several points on your lower body; usually at the groin, the top of the foot, and the inside of the ankle. Other symptoms will be watched for, such as an accumulation of fluids that could tip off the doctor to deep-system insufficiency.

At the groin, where the saphenous vein meets the femoral vein, the doctor will be feeling for blood flowing backward through the femoral valve. You'll be asked to cough—if the valve is functioning properly, there will be no backward flow. If the valve does open, the doctor will be able to feel it. That will tell the doctor to look closer for involvement of the long saphenous vein, and a possible surgical procedure.

The physician or physician's assistant may then mark the location of the visible varicose veins on the medical chart that will become a permanent part of your file.

Some doctors may amend the chart each time you visit, as a pictorial history of your case. Others may photograph your legs. Still others may order a number of further tests to map more accurately the problem areas.

TESTS

Probably 95% of patients who visit a varicose vein specialist will never have any tests other than a visual assessment and manual exam. That's because most varicose vein cases are quite simple and straightforward, and easily identifiable. But just in case a doctor sees something that brings up more questions than answers, there are a battery of tests at his disposal that can be used if need be. Here's a quick summary of the most widely used ones, how they work, and what they're supposed to do.

TRENDLENBURG'S TEST. The simplest test of the lower circulatory system—aside from just looking—requires no high-tech apparatus other than a rubber band. Trendlenburg's test (named after the physician who devised it in 1886) simply requires the patient to lie down and raise his or her leg for a few minutes to allow the blood to drain from the veins. The rubber band is used as a tourniquet on the upper thigh, sealing off the superficial veins from above. Then the patient stands up. If the varicose veins fill up within twenty or thirty seconds, it indicates faulty perforator veins—the blood must be coming from the deep system backward through the perforators to the superficial veins. If the veins don't fill in those few seconds, the tourniquet is released. If the long saphenous vein fills from above, that is, the blood coming backward from just above the tourniquet, then it's the culprit.

Particular faulty valves can then be found by a process of elimination, using tourniquets in tandem and repeating the test until the faulty valves are isolated from the functioning ones.

Other tests are sometimes used if the doctor suspects a problem more complex than common varicose veins. If deep-system obstructions are a possibility, **light reflective rheography** (light pletheismography) can be used to actually see into the deep-system vessels. A probe is taped to the leg in the area of the suspected obstruction, and the device records the filling and emptying of the capillaries by bouncing light impulses up through the tissues. From the graph the machine prints out, the physician can spot possible roadblocks deep in the leg. Rheography tells the physician the same kinds of things as the Trendlenburg test, but far more accurately.

Rarely, some doctors may use **venography**, an X-ray procedure that uses a dye to trace the vein network throughout the leg. Venography can show defective valves, faulty vessels, and obstructions of the deep system. This procedure will be done when the doctor suspects deep-system disease.

If a physician wants to know how much force is pushing the blood back to the heart, then he might ask for an **ambulatory venous pressure measurement**. Again, for most common varicose veins, this information is not necessary; only if the doctor suspects a more complicated circulatory problem might this test be used. A needle connected to a pressure recording device is inserted into a vein in the foot. Readings are taken both at rest and during exercise. In normal cases, venous pressure is high at rest and drops during activity. When there's a problem deep in the leg, the pressure stays high. (This test is considered obsolete, thanks to the advent of pletheismography and Doppler study.)

Doppler study is a test that uses ultrasound—very high frequency sound waves similar to radar—to track venous activity. Chances are great you'll never have one done, unless your problem is very unusual or of great magnitude.

After your physician has completed any tests he feels are necessary, he will have a good idea of the forces that are at work in your venous system, and that understanding will point him in the direction of a treatment program.

WHAT DO YOU WANT FROM TREATMENT?

This may seem to be an odd question. Most people who go to a doctor to be treated for varicose veins have had them for years, and are anxious to do something—anything—about them. Sure, they want the discomfort to stop. (That's no problem; stopping the discomfort is well within the abilities of medical science.) Yes, they want the disfiguring, ugly blue ribbons of protruding veins to go away. (Again, that's pretty easy if you find a qualified doctor.) But sometimes varicose vein patients get the idea that going to a doctor means that their legs will look just like they did when they were twenty years old. They might think that medical treatment is a fountain of youth.

Varicose vein therapy is not magic. It can do wonders for the physiological problems in the lower venous system, and the newest techniques can do some pretty amazing things with the cosmetic appearance of the affected areas. But no varicose vein treatment can correct the damage that may have occurred over years of circulatory insufficiency.

What are the symptoms that even the best treatment cannot cure? Sometimes varicose veins can begin to spontaneously bleed under the skin. The brown blotchy marks that can result can never be removed, because they are stains under the surface of the skin. The brown color comes from the iron that's present in the blood. Often, the affected area is discolored by edema and swelling, and it's not until after treatment—when the area returns to its normal coloration—that the stains become visible.

It's also important to remember that, unless a surgeon removes the long saphenous vein, the structural causes of varicose veins are still present. Treatment is not an inoculation against any future development of varicose veins; treatment only cures the varicose veins that are there, not those that might be varicose in the future. Remember: Varicose veins are caused by many things, most of which your doctor is powerless to do anything about—heredity, your occupation, your hormone levels, and so on. This simple fact comes as a shock to many patients, especially patients of sclerotherapy, who liken the injections to "shots" of anti-varicose vein vaccine. There is no "anti-varicose vein vaccine," and there is no known way to halt the process completely, other than to treat the existing varicosities. Surgery comes closest to halting the process if the cause is traced to the long saphenous vein. But if the root cause is mysterious (like the cause of most varicose veins is), your doctor can only treat the symptoms.

Then again, the formation of varicose veins is very slow. Symptomatic treatment may eliminate all the visible veins, and you may not live long enough for new ones to appear. For all practical purposes, you may never have a recurrence again.

The other possibility is that you may be disappointed. Most varicose vein sufferers must be prepared for a lifetime of caution and care. Their condition must be monitored, and they must be aware of any changes that may occur in their legs. Think of varicose veins like you think of tooth decay: while there are things you can do to prevent decay from happening, the forces that cause the decay are always there and cannot be completely halted. The key to successful treatment is awareness, prevention, and maintenance. The same goes for your legs.

Don't be put off by this warning, however. Of the thousands of patients who seek medical treatment for their varicose veins, the vast majority—over 90%—experience no significant recurrence of the condition over a period of years. However, there is the other side of that coin to contend with: not every patient is free from recurrence. Not every patient's definition of "significant" is the same, either. It's important for you to understand your own definition and to expect a realistic result from your treatment.

WHAT TECHNIQUE IS RIGHT FOR YOU?

It would be foolish for this book to recommend a specific procedure for you. There is, of course, no way for a book to do a physical examination, or to ask you about your medical history. It's the information that your doctor gets from you in these ways that guides him to a diagnosis and treatment program.

But this book can outline a few areas that should get you thinking about the possibilities.

Conservative, noninvasive techniques such as support hose, leg makeup, and preventative measures such as exercise are very valuable to slow the onset of varicose veins, or to ease their symptoms, without a lot of expense or bother. But these techniques can do nothing to remove or treat the varicosities you may already have. Those will be with you until you seek medical intervention from a doctor.

To the majority of varicose vein sufferers, those patients with the most common forms of varicose veins, modern sclerotherapy technique is definitely worth investigating. Ninety percent of all varicose vein cases can be treated effectively with sclerotherapy, yet this fact is not well known by the general public, or even by medical professionals not very familiar with varicose vein treatments. Ask your doctor about it. But don't be surprised if his opinion is based on some old information.

Surgery has really changed over the last twenty years. It used to be the only procedure accepted as truly effective by most physicians. Today it's seen as a procedure of last resort. When sclerotherapy is not effective—when the long saphenous vein of the leg is involved—then the long saphenous vein must be removed by the short, simple procedure, ligation and stripping. This technique has been around for some time, but only recently has it been refined to the point that the patient can be out of the hospital, walking under his or her own power, just two or three hours after leaving the operating room. The surgeon needs to make just two small incisions, which heal quickly and nearly invisibly, and the insufficient vessel is removed completely.

And if your physician recommends an electronic technique for the smallest spiders, look for the latest argon laser techniques, not the older forms of electrocautery or fulgaration procedures. Maybe the technology hasn't yet filtered out into the smaller cities, but at the very least your physician should be aware of the work that has been done in this field, and aware that you know a little about it, too.

HOW MUCH WILL IT COST?
WILL INSURANCE COVER YOUR TREATMENT?

It depends on your personal coverage. Though, if a broad generalization can be made, probably insurance will pay for a good deal of treatment.

Usually health insurance plans will provide for a percentage of the procedures. How much depends on your specific plan. Most plans will pay in the neighborhood of 80% of the cost, though some will pay for only 60%. Not only will you have to investigate your plan, but you'll have to consult with your physician about your diagnosis. Some plans may differentiate between strictly cosmetic treatments, such as for small spider veins, and physiologically important procedures, such as for larger varicosities that affect lower body circulation. Surgery, on the other hand, may be treated altogether differently.

Not too long ago, Blue Cross and Blue Shield, the biggest medical insurers who set the pace for many of the smaller companies, refused to cover any hospital procedures that didn't require an overnight stay. The advent of ambulatory surgery made that approach obsolete. Not only does ambulatory surgery save money for the patient, the hospital, and the insurance company, it means faster recovery, fewer patient complications, and more hospital beds available for the seriously ill. It's only recently that the insurance companies have started to come around on this issue, and by no means have all of them changed their policies. You'll have to investigate your own coverage to find out for sure.

SHOULD YOU GET A SECOND OPINION?

Second opinions are always a good idea. If you are well informed about your condition and know a little about options and other possibilities of treatment, this is a question you can answer yourself: Does your doctor's opinion sound reasonable to you? If it does, and if the treatment he suggests is not out of proportion to your condition, then you could risk not seeking out a second, perhaps confusing, opinion. The problem with second opinions is that if they don't agree with each other, you—someone who is not a doctor and only has a layman's limited understanding of the medical issues involved—are left to be the judge of what is the appropriate treatment.

If the second opinion agrees with the first . . . well, that's easy.

If it doesn't, that makes you the doctor.

Instead, listen carefully to the doctor. Is yours a common case, or something unusual? Is the doctor suggesting a treatment that sounds like overkill? Is the procedure he or she advocates as advanced as some you've heard about? If you are the least bit uncomfortable with any of the answers to questions like these, seek a second opinion. If you are at ease, and trust your physician, then maybe you can do without.

If you suffer from varicose veins, there is quite a lot that you can do for yourself. You can lose weight, you can quit smoking. You can exercise frequently, and you can elevate your legs at every opportunity. You can avoid tight-fitting clothes. You can eat more fiber.

But if you want actually to treat your varicose veins, remove and eliminate them, and (hopefully) keep them from coming back ever again, you've got to see a doctor. Only a doctor can prescribe therapy based on a diagnosis you're not qualified to make for yourself. Only a doctor can administer the simple—and effective— medications that can really make a big difference in the way you and your varicose veins look, and feel.

That's why it's crucial that all sufferers of varicose veins find physicians whom they trust. Physicians who know about the problems of varicose vein sufferers, both medically and emotionally. Physicians who know the most up-to-date methods and procedures, and have enough skill and fluency in all of these procedures to be able to pick the most appropriate form of treatment from among them, and to mix them effectively to suit a very specific sufferer of varicose veins—you.

PART III

PREVENTION AND MAINTENANCE

CHAPTER 10

LIVING WITH VARICOSE VEINS: DO'S AND DON'TS

If you've read this far, you've learned quite a bit of what medicine knows about the anatomy of varicose veins, their probable causes, the way doctors diagnose and treat the condition, and how you should go about choosing between the various treatments that are available.

But is that all there is?

Is there nothing you can do except watch varicose veins appear, then rush to your doctor to have them treated?

Isn't there anything you can do to actively manage your condition?

For years and years, the answer seemed to be no. Doctors didn't give any effective advice, and patients didn't ask. It seemed that no one really wanted to know. After all, most varicose veins didn't cause all that much trouble; they just looked bad. And there were more serious things for doctors to worry about other than a patient's vanity.

Today, fortunately, things have turned the other way. Varicose vein sufferers are speaking up, asking questions, and demanding the attention long due to them. In today's medical climate, the disfigurement of varicose veins is finally being seen as a medical condition worth talking about.

And that means more information—valuable, useful information—for the varicose vein sufferer. Information that can help you delay the progress of varicosities, keep them from getting worse, and make the varicose veins you might have more bearable.

Living with varicose veins means taking some precautions, and changing some habits. It means being aware that the things you do during the day can have an effect on the way you feel, and the way you look.

DON'T BE SEDENTARY

Since a varicose vein sufferer has circulatory problems, it's important that your daily activities don't make your body's job any tougher. It's the muscles that to a larger degree power the blood through the veins, so make sure you get enough physical exercise every day. There are specific exercises you can do to help yourself (see the next chapter), and you might want to incorporate these into your daily routine. But even when you're not exercising—while at work or at home, riding in a car or plane, even while lying in bed—there are some "mini-exercises" you can do all during the day. These simple techniques can help you to keep your muscles taut and firm, so that they'll move your blood around more efficiently.

Do move your feet up and down, heel to toe, as if

you were pumping a piano pedal, or keeping time to music, while sitting or standing for long periods of time. Alternate feet, for a few minutes each.

Do wriggle your toes frequently and forcefully.

Do quick sidesteps under your desk, or as you stand in place.

Do swing your feet back and forth, side to side.

Do stretch out your legs, then draw them back up.

Do walk as much as possible, even if it's only around the room, for a few minutes every hour. Almost anybody can walk, no matter how old one is. Try to walk as fast as is comfortable for you.

Do put your legs up as much as you can, especially if you're resting for a while. Cross your legs only at the ankles, not the knees. If you can, lie down, with your legs higher than your heart.

Don't sit still, or stand in one place for any length of time. The force of gravity causes blood and other fluids to collect in your legs, and that's what causes, aggravates, and accelerates varicose veins.

WATCH YOUR WEIGHT AND WHAT YOU EAT

If you are susceptible to varicose veins, obesity can make the problem worse. After all, fat people have more blood, and more (and larger) cells to feed. But they have the same number of veins as a thin person, and a smaller muscle-to-body-weight ratio. That means more work for those veins, with less help. And less support from the surrounding tissues.

Don't eat fattening, fatty, salty, low-fiber foods. They all promote weight gain. Not only that, but low-fiber foods can cause chronic constipation, which can strain the entire lower circulatory system and cause hemorrhoids to boot. Over a period of many years, this can lead to a breakdown of veins and valves, and varicosities can result.

Do eat a diet that's high in fiber, low in salt and sugar. Whole grains, such as oats, barley, brown rice, and whole wheat, contain the raw materials to keep your system functioning smoothly. Eat fresh vegetables and fruits; avoid sweets, pastries and soft drinks with sugar, and fats. (It's better for your heart, too.) Cultures whose diets are high in foods like these have a markedly lower incidence of varicose veins; yet, when these people move to industrialized nations with low-fiber, high-fat diets, their incidence catches up within two generations.

Do maintain proper body weight. In order to be successfully treated for varicose veins, you should weigh within 10% of your ideal body weight. There are several reasons. Excess weight strains an already burdened circulatory system, as we've noted. Losing weight will reduce the pressures on your veins, and give your doctor a much better idea of the extent of your problem. Depending on the treatment, excess body fat can be a hinderance to the procedure, limiting your doctor's options, and perhaps resulting in a less than ideal outcome.

Don't lose weight quickly on a fad diet. It won't work. Relapse rates for crash diets are high, and the effects on your body can be hazardous. If you need to slim down, do it slowly and steadily over a period of months. This method is safer, and more reliable, with more permanent results.

WATCH WHAT YOU WEAR

Don't interfere with your own circulatory system by placing obstacles between your legs and your heart. Some of what passes for fashionable garments are only that; these garments can slow down the flow of blood, causing fluids to collect in the lower legs, aggravating varicose vein problems.

Don't wear constricting garments such as girdles, garters, tight belts, snug pants, etc., unless, as in the case of support stockings, your doctor prescribes them. High heels are fine, however; they seem to have absolutely no effect on a varicose vein condition.

Do wear loose-fitting, comfortable clothing that doesn't bind or constrict, especially in the areas of the waist, groin, and lower abdomen.

BE ESPECIALLY AWARE THAT PREGNANCY MAY CAUSE VARICOSE VEINS

Most women who suffer from varicose veins can trace their origins back to pregnancies. The reasons, previously discussed, have to do with the increase in blood volume, the pressure of the growing uterus on the veins of the lower body that pass near it, and the increased levels of hormones in a pregnant woman's body. And since heredity determines, to a large degree, whether you are predisposed to developing varicose veins, find out your own family history. If varicose veins are present, be especially vigilant.

Do get plenty of appropriate exercise during your pregnancy.

Do eat a low-salt, high-fiber diet. Avoid constipation if at all possible.

Do wear loose clothing, and follow all the other cautions you would normally follow.

DON'T TAKE THE PILL

Since pregnancy itself is so instrumental in the onset of varicose veins, it only stands to reason that oral contraceptives—which work by fooling your body into thinking it's pregnant when it's not—promote and aggravate varicose veins, too. The hormones that your body produces during pregnancy, estrogen and progesterone, are the main ingredients of birth control pills. The link between the Pill and circulatory problems like blood clots and varicose veins is clear. If you think you are developing varicose veins, or might be predisposed to them, find another safe method of contraception.

DO TAKE CARE OF YOURSELF

If you are predisposed to varicose veins, keep an eye out for them. Look for warning signs, like dull throbbing pain in the lower legs toward the end of the day, telltale discolorations, or swellings. If you find developing varicose veins, or if you've had them for a while, examine yourself regularly for any changes or worsening of the condition.

Do protect your legs. Keep your toenails clean and clipped, apply baby powder after bathing to protect the skin and, during dry weather especially, use a moisturizer on your legs to keep the skin from cracking. A serious problem for varicose vein sufferers, especially those with advanced cases, is a general deterioration of the skin on the lower legs, due to the accumulation of fluids. Keep a sharp lookout for any injury that heals slowly; it could be the beginning of an ulceration.

Don't ignore any small sore that doesn't heal quickly. If you suspect an ulcer might be forming, call your doctor immediately. If an ulcer is left untreated, serious complications can result.

Do seek treatment as soon as possible for any condition you suspect is varicose veins. Remember, once you have varicose veins, they won't go away by themselves, but you can slow down their development if you seek medical help early. It's important to halt their progress before complications occur, like swelling, discoloration of the skin, ulcers, dermatitis, bleeding, and, in serious cases, thrombophlebitis—an inflamed vein that causes blood clots to form. The sooner you go to the doctor, the better the results will be after treatment.

CHAPTER 11

EXERCISE CAN HELP

When it comes to varicose veins, exercise is a form of "preventive maintenance" that can effectively invigorate the circulatory system, making the veins in the legs more efficient. This doesn't mean that exercise can make your existing varicose veins go away; only appropriate medical treatment can do that. But exercising on a regular basis *can* help you prevent the condition from worsening, and it can help you manage the pain and discomfort of varicose veins, too.

We said in Chapter 1 that the muscle pump is an important force in moving the blood from the limbs to the heart. In the physically inactive person with varicose veins, the efficiency of the muscle pump is often compromised because the muscles themselves lack the tone and strength to propel the blood at a sufficient rate. Combine that problem with the inefficiency of the veins themselves, with their malfunctioning valves and improper directional flow—and you've got a poorly maintained machine doing a less-than-adequate job.

Exercise's contribution can be dramatic. One survey[13] found that almost 75% of people who have successfully coped with varicose veins got substantial benefits from exercising, from walking to swimming, to calisthenics, even to belly-dancing. And exercise doesn't have to be a painful, brutal experience, either. Just a sane, reasonable program that mixes aerobic activities like walking, bicycling, or swimming with a few well-chosen calisthenics can tone up your muscles enough to improve your circulatory picture markedly.

STARTING OUT: TAKE A WALK

One exercise nearly everyone can do, regardless of age or state of health, is vigorous walking. (If you are not steady enough on your feet for a brisk walk, start with a slow one instead.) Walking is called a perfect exercise, because it uses all the muscles of the lower body, and quite a few in the upper body as well, and it uses them in a natural way that isn't likely to cause injuries, no matter how inexperienced you are.

Start your walking regimen by taking a brisk walk for only a few minutes the first day, gradually going longer and longer distances. Find a pace that just begins to work up a slight sweat, and stay with it.

Varicose vein treatment has always included walking as therapy, usually in conjunction with other therapies or techniques, such as sclerotherapy or surgery. Researchers have found that the activity of walking several miles a day has improved recovery time, and that those patients who continued the walking as an everyday activity beyond their recoveries, had fewer continuing problems.

JOGGING AND RUNNING. More vigorous than walking is jogging and running. Again, start very slowly, building up your routine as you build your stamina. Jog around the block the first week, then gradually add a few minutes to your workout every week.

If you've been essentially inactive or if you have any other health concerns, see your doctor before you embark on a running program. Running is potentially dangerous if you have a history of heart trouble, arthritis, or past injuries. But if you are otherwise healthy and your doctor approves, running can be an excellent way to dramatically improve your physical fitness along with your circulation. Many people are devoted to it, and there are numerous books that expound on the physical, and some say spiritual, aspects of running.

BICYCLING AND SWIMMING. These two sports also offer substantial benefits to the varicose vein sufferer, though for best results, they should be part of a regular routine.

Bicycling, like walking, is a perfect activity in that it gives each part of your body exercise, while sparing it the bone-jarring punishment of other sports, like jogging or tennis. Bicycling also has the advantage of being a pleasant form of transportation and an excellent form of sightseeing, so you can get your exercise while enjoying the world around you.

Swimming works every part of your body, too, with little or no inappropriate stress on any one part. Swim laps in a large enough body of water so you can work up your heart rate, then continue the activity for as long as is comfortable. Gradually add more laps as your stamina increases.

ANY SPORT THAT USES YOUR WHOLE BODY IS GOOD. That includes tennis, basketball, soccer, raquetball, volleyball, and squash. Also activities like dancing, hiking, skiing, or even mountain-climbing. The important thing is to get moving, and to keep moving, at least three times a week.

THE VARICOSE VEIN EXERCISE PROGRAM

Created with the assistance of sports physiologist Matthew Collelo.
Fourteen exercises that will strengthen and tone your legs and buttocks and improve circulation in your legs.

While general physical activity can have an overall beneficial effect on the state of your health and the condition of your circulatory system, specific exercises, custom-made for the muscles in the varicose-vein prone areas, can have an even more direct effect on improving the function of specific problem veins.

Any exercise that firms and strengthens the calves, thighs, and buttocks—the key components of the muscle pump in the lower body—can have a beneficial effect on circulation in these problem areas. We've chosen the following exercises because, if performed regularly, they can help tone the varicose vein areas and improve the condition of the muscle pump where it will do the most good.

Each exercise is preceded by a brief explanation of the muscles involved, and the number of times you should repeat the exercise to achieve an effective result.

Nine of the exercises are simple enough to be performed in your home without any elaborate equipment. But because so many people today have access to body-building equipment at the gym, or even at home, you'll find five exercises that can be performed on common exercise machines.

When you exercise at home, you should try to arrange for a daily workout, as it's the repetition of the exercises over a period of time that makes them effective. Do them in the order that they appear here, for the suggested number of repetitions, in a slow and deliberate fashion.

Once the exercises become easy to do, you can carefully increase the degree of difficulty by doing **one** of these things:

- go through the exercises more than once
- increase the number of repetitions in each exercise
- add ankle weights of 2½ pounds to each foot

THE SQUAT

Muscles involved: Thighs and Buttocks

Repetitions: 15–20

1. Stand upright, with your feet about a foot apart, toes angled slightly outward.
2. Put your arms straight out to the front, parallel to the floor. Focus your eyes on your fingertips and keep them there throughout the exercise.
3. Slowly lower your body by bending your knees. Keep your torso and head straight. Lower your body into a squatting position.
4. Once your thighs are parallel to the floor, return to an upright position. Repeat 15–20 times.

(If you find it hard to balance during this exercise, try placing a plank or similar object under your heels.)

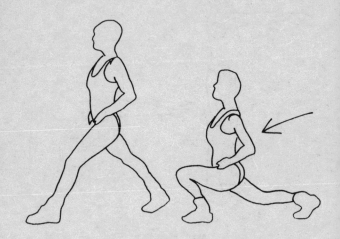

THE LUNGE

Muscles involved: Thighs and Buttocks

Repetitions: 10–15 each leg.

1. Stand upright, hands on hips. Place your left foot about 3 feet in front of your right foot, as if you were taking a long step.
2. Make sure your left foot is flat on the floor. Your right foot should be resting on its ball.
3. Lunge forward by bending the left knee. Keep your body and head upright.
4. When the right knee is almost on the floor, return to the starting position. Repeat this movement 10–15 times, then alternate legs and repeat.

BACK LEG EXTENSION

Muscles involved: Buttocks and Hamstrings

Repetitions: 10–15

1. Position yourself on hands and knees, with your knees apart by the width of your body.
2. Extend your left leg straight behind you, with toes pointed.
3. Lift your extended leg as high as you can, stretching up toward the ceiling.
4. Lower it slowly, keeping it straight. Remember to keep your head up and your arms straight.
5. Repeat 10–15 times, then alternate legs and repeat.

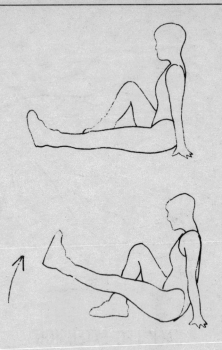

SITTING LEG RAISE

Muscles involved: Quadriceps and Hip Flexors

Repetitions: 10–15

1. Sit on the floor, arms at your side and legs extended straight out in front of you.
2. By bending your right knee, place your right foot flat on the floor next to your left knee.
3. Now flex your left foot and raise your left leg up without bending the knee.
4. Lower it slowly, but don't touch the floor. Repeat 10–15 times, alternate legs and repeat.

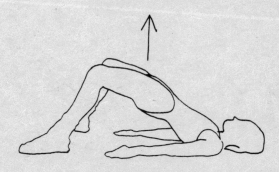

PELVIC LIFT

Muscles involved: Buttocks, Hamstrings, and Lower Back

Repetitions: 10–15

1. Lie on your back, with your arms lying alongside your body, and your knees bent. Spread your feet apart a little more than the width of your body.
2. Flex your buttocks tightly, and lift toward the ceiling, as if an invisible rope were picking you up from the middle of your body.
3. Lower yourself slowly, coming to rest on the floor. Repeat 10–15 times.

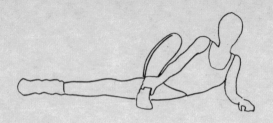

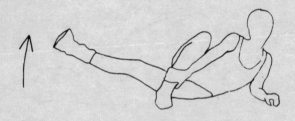

INNER THIGH LIFTS

Muscles involved: Adductors

Repetitions: 10–15

1. Lie on your left side, leaning on your left elbow, with your legs extending straight on a line with your torso.
2. Grasp your right foot with your right hand. Place your right foot flat on the floor in front of your left knee. You'll look a little like a pretzel.
3. With your left foot flexed, lift your left leg straight up, toward the ceiling. Lower it slightly between lifts, repeating 10–15 times.
4. Alternate legs and repeat.

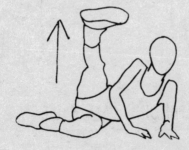

OUTER THIGH LIFTS

Muscles involved: Abductors

Repetitions: 10–15

1. Lie on your left side, up on your left elbow, with your palms flat on the floor.
2. Fold knees toward your chest. Extend right leg out straight, with foot flexed, so it is perpendicular to your body. Make sure you maintain this perpendicular position.
3. Lift your right leg up toward the ceiling, and then lower it slowly to the floor, but not letting it touch. Repeat 10–15 times, then alternate legs and repeat.

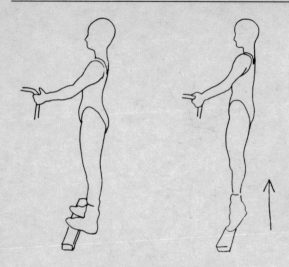

STANDING CALF RAISE

Muscles involved: Calves

Repetitions: 15–20

1. You'll need a thick telephone book, or a length of two-by-four lumber, for this exercise, as well as a chair.

   Stand with your toes and balls of your feet on the telephone book or wood. Spread your feet about 8–10 inches apart, toes pointed straight ahead. Hold onto the back of a chair for balance.
2. Standing upright, lower your heels until they are below your toes. The lower your heels can go, the better.
3. Now keeping your legs straight, raise yourself as high as you can by standing on your toes. Then lower your heels slowly to the starting position. Repeat 15–20 times.

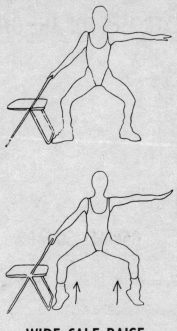

WIDE CALF RAISE

Muscles involved: Calves

Repetitions: 15–20

1. You will need a chair for this exercise.
    Stand with your legs as wide apart as you can, toes pointed out. The wider you can go, the better.
2. Lower your buttocks toward the floor by bending your knees, until your buttocks are slightly higher than your knees. Hold onto a chair back for balance.
3. Raise your heels as high as you can, then lower them to the floor. Repeat 15–20 times.

EXERCISES FOR THE GYM

BARBELL SQUAT

Muscles involved: Thighs and Buttocks

Repetitions: 15–20

1. Place a barbell behind your head, resting the bar above the shoulder blades. Use a comfortable weight, not one that's too heavy. Ask a qualified trainer for assistance in selecting a weight that's right for you.
2. Slowly bend your knees and lower your body into a squat position. Make sure you keep your body upright, and your head straight, eyes fixed on an imaginary point at about shoulder height.
3. When your thighs are parallel to the floor, return to starting position. Repeat 15–20 times.

    You may find it difficult to maintain your balance during this exercise. Try placing a board or similar flat object about 1–2 inches high under your heels.

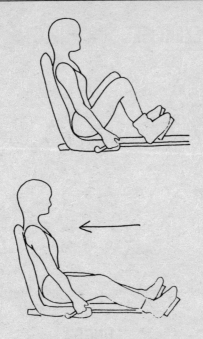

LEG PRESS MACHINE

Muscles involved: Thighs and Buttocks

Repetitions: 12–15

1. Adjust the moveable seat forward or backward so that when you are seated, your knees are bent 90 degrees.
2. Sitting upright in the seat, grasp the handles at the sides of the seat, and place your feet flat against the pedals in front of you.
3. Straighten your legs slowly, allowing for a slight bend at the knee. Bend legs back to starting position and repeat 12–15 times.

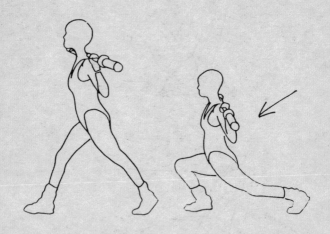

LUNGE

Muscles involved: Thighs and Buttocks

Repetitions: 10–15

1. Place a barbell behind your head, resting it on your shoulder blades. Place one foot about 3 feet in front of the other, the foot flat on the floor. Let your rear foot rest on its ball and toe.
2. Lunge your body forward by bending your front-most knee. Be sure to keep your torso upright and head straight.
3. Once the rear leg is close to the floor, return to the starting position. Repeat 10–15 times, alternate legs, and repeat.

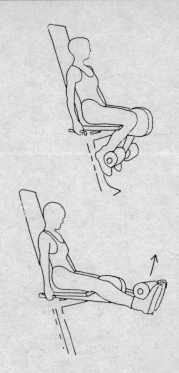

LEG EXTENSION MACHINE

Muscles involved: Quadriceps

Repetitions: 12–15

1. In the seated position, place your feet behind the roller pads.
2. Straighten your legs to their fully flexed position, and pause.
3. Slowly lower your legs. Repeat 12–15 times, but don't let the weights rest.

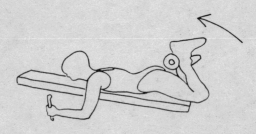

LEG CURL MACHINE

Muscles involved: Hamstrings

Repetitions: 12–15

1. Lie face down on the machine, with your knees just off the edge of the bench. Place feet under the roller pads.
2. Bend your legs at the knee, trying to bring your heels to your buttocks.
3. Slowly lower your legs and repeat 12–15 times.

PART IV

RESOURCES

APPENDIX 1

PRODUCTS YOU
MIGHT FIND HELPFUL

If you suffer from varicose veins (and if you've read through most of this book), you probably realize that there is no one right way to cope with the problem. Medical treatment is certainly an important part of living with varicose veins, but as we've discussed at length, it's not the only part. There are things you can do for yourself either before you see a doctor or after you've consulted with one—including the use of various products made just for varicose vein patients.

This part of the book is a guide to those products. Some, namely medical support hose, will require a doctor's prescription. There are patients, particularly obese people or those with serious venous insufficiencies, such as edema or leg ulcers, who may require custom-made products. Other products, such as make-ups that hide the ugly blue lines and spider veins that mark the varicose vein sufferer, or sunscreens for patients undergoing sclerotherapy or electronic therapies, are available in most drugstores or through the mail.

SUPPORT STOCKINGS

The theory behind support stockings is simple: By compressing the veins of the legs, they keep blood from collecting in distended areas of the varicose veins. Circulation is improved, fluids are kept from accumulating in the tissues of lower legs, so you feel better. It's not an invasive procedure to correct the basic problem of varicose veins, but rather a maintenance technique with low-risk at a modest cost. For people who are not well enough to undergo any other procedures for their varicose veins, or who for some reason do not wish to treat them in other ways, support stockings offer a stop-gap measure that give fairly good results under certain conditions.

So why doesn't everybody just wear support hose and happily live ever after with varicose veins? Because the drawbacks of depending on support hose are substantial over a long period of time.

First of all, support stockings are uncomfortable. They're hot and itchy in warm weather, irritate the skin and generally make a nuisance of themselves.

And they're usually ugly. That may be changing these days, gradually, but you'll never find the choice of styles, colors, and sizes that regular pantyhose is widely available in.

They wear out, but not the way ordinary pantyhose does. With support stockings, the degree of compression gradually fades, so you can never be really sure if they're still effective.

And there's quite a routine involved in putting them on, taking them off, and caring for them. Refer to Part II, Chapter 1 in this book for a brief description of how support stockings are applied.

Lastly, and most importantly, support stockings do not, in any way, cure the underlying varicose vein condition. If you have varicose veins and wear support stockings, you will still have the same varicose veins when you take those support stockings off. They are not effective for controlling spider veins. There is the suggestion that wearing support stockings can slow the progress of a developing varicose vein condition, and might slow down the advent of complications as well, but support stockings don't fix the problem. They can only make it feel better temporarily.

Medical support hose are a very different garment from the support hose you can buy in a department store. Medical support hose have much greater compression power than the over-the-counter variety of support hose. Those are lightweight stockings, which may have a gently therapeutic effect on the average wearer; they're best at things such as helping to relieve leg fatigue. The principle by which they work is similar to that of medical support hose; it's mostly a matter of degree. The idea behind medical support hose is to prevent blood from accumulating in the tissues of the lower leg, by keeping the veins compressed throughout the day. Blood can't pool in distended veins if the veins aren't distended.

In order to accomplish this, medical support stockings are graduated; that is, the compression is greatest at the ankle and becomes gradually less as the stocking goes to the thigh. This graduated compression not only keeps the veins from filling up, but it also helps the pumping action of the leg muscles return the blood to the heart.

Too much compression, though, could actually hinder the circulation and make matters worse. Too little wouldn't do much of anything. So graduated support stockings are available in various strengths—as defined in millimeters of mercury (mm Hg), a measure of pressure—and are available by prescription only.

Here are some general guidelines for degrees of compression.

20–30 mm Hg: Will relieve feelings of heaviness and fatigue in the leg, and is effective in cases of mild varicosities without any sign of accompanying edema. Often prescribed for women with mild varicose veins during pregnancy.

30–40 mm Hg: Used for the relief of aching, more serious fatigue and feelings of heaviness. Might be prescribed for pregnant patients who have had previous serious varicosities with accompanying venous inflammation or phlebitis, or for patients with edema and developing stasis dermatitis. In general, 30–40 mm Hg stockings are the most commonly prescribed support hose.

40–50 mm Hg: For severe cases of varicosity, edema with stasis dermatitis, and other complications of venous insufficiency.

50–60 mm Hg: Used for the most severe cases where the integrity of the deep venous system is seriously impaired, such as in cases of post-thrombotic syndrome.

This class of stockings, 40–60 mm Hg, is usually reserved for patients with severe complications of the lower circulatory system. The stockings are designed not for comfort or attractiveness, but rather for the serious job of controlling serious problems. They're no-nonsense medical tools to be used under very specific circumstances.

Support hose are available in many different styles, from many different manufacturers. They are often intended to be worn under regular nylon stockings, but some manufacturers have attempted to make the more moderate grades of hose somewhat "normal" looking, offering sheer styles and a selection of colors. Some manufacturers will make support stockings to the individual patient's measurements, though more and more of the manufacturers are making so many slightly different sizes that their "off the shelf" hose are very nearly as good-fitting as their custom-made brethren.

Most major manufacturers of support hosiery offer similar lines of products. Following is the sort of variety most manufacturers offer to doctors for distribution to their patients *by prescription only*. **NOTE: Federal law restricts these devices to sale by or on the order of a physician.**

- **Below-the-knee styles**

- **Mid thigh**

- **Full thigh**

- **Pantyhose with variations for different body shapes and conditions**

- **Different grades of compression for all of the above styles**

- **Some variety of colors for select styles (usually tan, white, sometimes black or nude)**

- **Sheer pantyhose and knee-highs, perhaps in several colors**

- **Maternity pantyhose in a variety of sizes**

- **Men's support hose, perhaps in both a heavy and light weight, in a variety of colors such as black, brown, navy, and white.**

MANUFACTURERS OF SUPPORT HOSIERY

RECOMMENDED:

Sigvaris (distributed by Camp International)
P.O. Box 89
Jackson, MI 49204

Black and Bauer
Becton Dickinson Consumer Products
One Becton Drive
Franklin Lakes, NY 07417

Bell-Horn and Brothers
451 N. Third St.
Philadelphia, PA 19123

Jobst Institute
Box 653
Toledo, OH 43694

VenES
Futuro
Jung Medical Products
5801 Mariemont Ave.
Cincinnati, OH 45227

CORRECTIVE MAKEUP

Many varicose vein sufferers use corrective makeup
to hide unsightly spider veins and true varicosities in
lieu of medical treatment. Several manufacturers offer

heavy-duty, waterproof, opaque makeups that can make discolorations due to varicosities "disappear." Makeups come in a variety of shades, which can be blended to match your skin tone. Application often takes practice to achieve a natural effect, but once applied, makeup can last for several days, through swimming and even bathing, as long as the area is not scrubbed with soap.

Following is a list of major manufacturers of corrective makeup for varicose vein sufferers.

Covermark by Lydia O'Leary
201 Route 17 North
Rutherford, NJ 07070
(Generally considered to be the best-known and most respected product in this category)

Natural Cover by Linda Seidel (mail-order only)
Box 21461
Pikesville, MD 21208

Amica Perfect Leg Cover
Custom Cosmetics Company
736 Parkside Avenue
Brooklyn, NY 11226

PROTECTIVE TANNING PRODUCTS

After sclerotherapy, the use of a suncare product is usually recommended, since there is a possibility that the sun might cause pigmentation and discoloration of the area. (In fact, exposure to the sun during any healing process is likely to cause a discoloration as melanin concentrates in the sensitive area.) The degree of protection is indicated by a Sun Protection Factor (SPF) number; the higher the number, the greater the protection. The highest SPF is normally around 15, although this can vary from brand to brand. Some brands now go as high as 22. A high SPF number indicates that the product is a sunblock and will afford maximum protection.

Most manufacturers produce sunblock sticks as well as creams. All are available over-the-counter products. These waterproof, lightweight sticks are recommended for touch-ups of those parts of the body most vulnerable to sun exposure. Broad spectrum sunscreens are available that according to studies conducted by the Pennsylvania School for Medicine, not only help prevent sunburn, but also work to promote repair of sun-damaged skin. There are also sunblocks designed for specific body parts, such as Coppertone's **For Faces Only** and Bain de Soleil's **Under Eye 15**. Other maximum protection products available in sticks and creams are: **Presun 15** by Westwood; **Sundown 15** and **Shade 15** by Coppertone; and **Eclipse 15** by Dorsey Laboratories.

For people with ultrasensitive skin or with a specific allergy to PABA (para-aminobenzoic acid), which is contained in all the screens mentioned above, Piz Buin manufactures a full line of non-allergenic broad-spectrum suncare products. In addition to creams and sticks ranging from SPF4 to 12, this European company also makes a total sunblock designed to withhold all ultraviolet rays from sensitive or damaged skin. (For more information, write to: Piz Buin North America; 1600 Two Turtle Creek Village; Dallas, TX 75219.)

APPENDIX 2

WHO TO CALL

Generally, the best place to look for a doctor to treat your varicose veins is in your own backyard: before turning anywhere else, call your regular physician (your regular physician is probably more familiar with your overall medical condition than anyone else); your local medical society (an organization of all the doctors in your area); or a nearby university hospital (university hospitals teach the latest medical techniques to new doctors) for a referral. But there may be cases when these local sources are unable to help you, and we therefore provide the addresses and/or phone numbers of the following national medical organizations to help you in your search:

International Cardiovascular Society
North American Chapter
13 Elm Street
Manchester, MA 01944
(617) 927-8330

Society of Vascular Surgery
(Dr. Wesley Moore)
(213) 825-9641

American Academy of Dermatology
(312) 869-3954

Things have changed quickly in the field of varicose vein treatment in the last five years, even over the last year. The new techniques are not only more effective than the old techniques, they make you look better than the old techniques ever could. That's why you should seek them out. It might be a little extra work, but your legs will love you for it.

FOOTNOTES

1. Primary Cardiology Journal, July 1983, p. 99, Malcolm O. Perry, M.D.

2. Textbook of Surgery, 1986, W. B. Saunders.

3. Alexander, Colin James, The Lancet, April 15, 1972, p. 822.

4. Fitzgerald, Graor, Lofgren, Smith III, M.D.s, Patient Care, March 30, 1984, p. 26.

5. Vascular Disorders of the Extremities, David I. Abrahamson, Harper and Row, 1974, p. 516.

6. Vascular Disorders of the Extremities, David I. Abrahamson, Harper and Row, 1974, p. 517.

7. Navarro's opinion.

8. Nabatoff, Ambulatory Surgery: Experience with 2000 Patients.

9. K.M. Douglas, G. Fischer, D. Reeleder, Compression Sclerotherapy for Varicose Veins, A Canadian Study, CMA Journal, Vol. 126, April 15, 1982, pp. 923–927.

10. Douglas, Fischer, Reeleder, Op Cit, p. 923.

11. J.A. Dormandy, A.B. Woodyer, A Randomised Trial of Bandaging After Sclerotherapy for Varicose Veins, Phlebologie 35 (1), 1982, pp. 125–131.

12. Sladen, Joseph G., M.D., Compression Sclerotherapy: Preparation, Technique, Complications and Results, The American Journal of Surgery, August 1983, pp. 228–229.

13. *Prevention* Magazine, August 1985, pp. 68–71.

ABOUT THE AUTHORS

Luis Navarro, M.D. is the founder and director of The Vein Treatment Center in New York City and an expert in the treatment of varicose veins. A board-certified general surgeon, he has devoted his practice exclusively to varicose vein problems. Dr. Navarro is a senior clinical instructor in surgery at The Mount Sinai School of Medicine. He also is affiliated with Beth Israel Medical Center and Lenox Hill Hospitals in Manhattan.

A cum laude graduate of the University of Barcelona in his native Spain, Dr. Navarro completed his post-graduate training and specialization at New York's Mount Sinai Medical Center. Dr. Navarro practiced general surgery with a special emphasis in varicose veins. In recognition of a growing need, in 1984 he founded The Vein Treatment Center, a facility that exclusively treats varicose veins and spider veins, from both a physiological and cosmetic point of view. At The Vein Treatment Center, Dr. Navarro conducts ongoing clinical research into the retardation and elimination of varicose veins.

Dr. Navarro's successful approach to the treatment of varicose veins is based on the principle of Combined Therapies which brings together new medical and surgical procedures, as well as refinements on classical techniques.

Nancy S. Miller and Stephen Kling are a husband and wife writing team. They live in New York with their two children.

BANTAM
SHOP-AT-HOME
C·A·T·A·L·O·G

Special Offer
Buy a Bantam Book
for only 50¢.

Now you can have Bantam's catalog filled with hundreds of titles plus take advantage of our unique and exciting bonus book offer. A special offer which gives you the opportunity to purchase a Bantam book for only 50¢. Here's how!

By ordering any five books at the regular price per order, you can also choose any other single book listed (up to a $5.95 value) for just 50¢. Some restrictions do apply, but for further details why not send for Bantam's catalog of titles today!

Just send us your name and address and we will send you a catalog!

Think of it as a Nutritional Insurance Policy

JEAN CARPER'S TOTAL NUTRITION GUIDE:

The Complete Official Report On Healthful Eating
☐ #34350-5 $12.95/$15.95 in Canada

No matter which diet you are on.
No matter which cuisine you favor.
In these health-conscious times you owe it to yourself and
your family to make sure that the food you eat is providing
the nutrition value you need.

JEAN CARPER'S TOTAL NUTRITION GUIDE is the most up-
to-date, authoritative guide to the nutritional value of the
foods we eat today. Based on the U.S.D.A.'s newest 10-year
scientific study of the nutritional content of food, *JEAN
CARPER'S TOTAL NUTRITION GUIDE* gives you the hard
facts on:

* nutritional guidelines for men, women, and children of
  all ages
* how too much or too little of some nutrients can affect
  your health
* HOW TO GET THE MOST NUTRIENTS FOR THE FEWEST
  CALORIES!

AND DON'T FORGET JEAN CARPER'S PERENNIAL BEST-
SELLERS NOW FULLY REVISED AND UPDATED:

☐ **THE ALL-IN-ONE CALORIE COUNTER** #26326 $4.50/
$5.50 in Canada
Complete and instant information on brand names, fresh
foods, health foods, low-cal foods and restaurant and
Fast foods.

☐ **THE ALL-IN-ONE CARBOHYDRATE GRAM COUNTER**
#26405-2 $4.50/$5.50 in Canada
Over 5,500 entries covering every type of prepared and
fresh food imaginable. The perfect companion for a high-
carbohydrate dieter.

Wherever Bantam books are sold or use the handy coupon
below:
- -